Random Thoughts V.4.1

365 UNREAD POEMS

Part One: The Autumn of Dreams

A Personal Journey in Poems and Photos

by

B. C. Baronia

Published by B.C. Publishing

ISBN: 978-1-7343041-2-1

About this Book Series

This book series was conceptualized in September 2017 after the publication of my second book of *Random Thoughts - Walk to Freedom*. I wrote about any topic my brain and – heart – would take an interest, sporadically that is, using my mobile phone *Notes*^{R}*. I then realized, I already have a ton of free verses distinct from my earlier haikus. This time, I thought I should also include photos I took before my *NYIP*** certification, now with a tweak – pictures in black and white using the built-in filters alongside the 365 poems! Daunting yet possible. With such a lofty dream and immense challenge, my imagination functioned like before. I am now convinced to share this book entitled "*365 Unread Poems" volume 4 of my Random Thoughts* into 4 series representing the 4 seasons in North America where I have lived for years.

This is *The Autumn of Dreams*, first of the 4 series.

Enjoy the read and the - ride.

B. C. Baronia

**Notes*^{R}, an app in an *iPhone* mobile phone, an *Apple* product.

***New York Institute of Photography*

"To those reading this book, I am speaking to y'all in 365 ways."

Foreword

With the digital form of communication comes a prize.

A wide gamut of choices is on hand - *read, save, copy, forward, reply, junk, trash, block, delete, delete without reading,* and more. I am an active *spectator* who has seen and touched *Broca's* and *Wernicke's* areas, classically designated as language-sensitive parts of the human brain, so I dare not muddle their function. When these areas or their fiber bundles are stimulated and results in transient loss of language, I beg y'all, let us keep our option with our language interaction to just one, **'reply'**. Breach not our covenant to anyone who interacts with us even in any form. Respond as we did in the past. Or else, we lose that vital part of being human, the *why* of our unique creation remains unread.

Thank y'all.

B.C.B.
15 Oct 2019

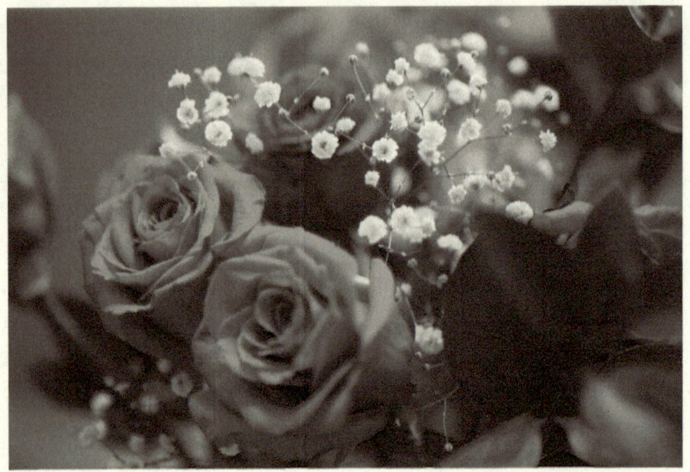

Hamilton, Ontario, Canada

Day *1 / 22 September*

Days in Advance

(Written intended for November 2)

I know you didn't hear
my thunderous whisper.
Didn't notice the taps of
my pointe shoes!

One hundred minus one,
you heed Peter's deed!
With one keyboard stroke,
my message floats!

There's a ghost in the air,
I know nothing but I despair!
This day I will always remember,
DD19, a day in red, not in amber!

A wish for your special day,
a best life with your family,
a joy with no end, an end to sigh.
A big smile only from a saintly one!

There's the boat at bay,
with the last straws of hay,
as summer jumps to winter,
Ahhh, I'll see you with the stars!

Double Meanings

(Read all the 2nd Word vertically from
top to bottom with each space as a paragraph break.)

To Look the way before.
To feel what I can't say.
To love with no end.

To Bring joy every time.
To smile with each sigh.

To Let her enjoy forever.
To dream as ever before.
To tell no one but oneself.

To Live each day as if it's last.
To care with every move.
To hope for every turn.

To Be happy as I was.
To firm up one's stand.

To Hide what I meant.

Day 2 / 23 September

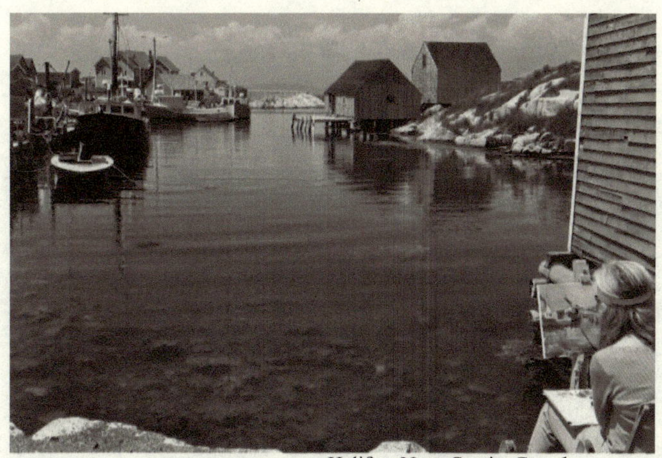

Halifax, Nova Scotia, Canada

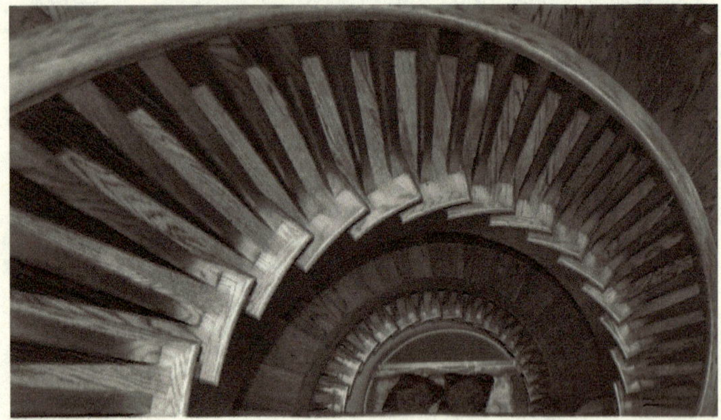

Hamilton, Ontario, Canada

Day 3 / 24 September

An Alternate Life's Recipe

To learn to be the best,
Much easier is to do the least.
To care for someone,
Like extended loved ones.
To succeed with awe,
bulls-eye's tight, aim for the side.
To wish for the star,
Close one's eyes and look far.
To live on a dream,
Be happy, live on La la land!

Let Me Fly with Our Words

As I read thru old texts
They filled up my heart,
Freshened up my mind,
Perked up my spirit!

They were digital records
Not just blips for passing.
They're personal resolve
of a future to behold.

It may not come so soon
But like the wind of joy
When it flies out there
I'll be with it, gone forever.

Day 4 / 25 September

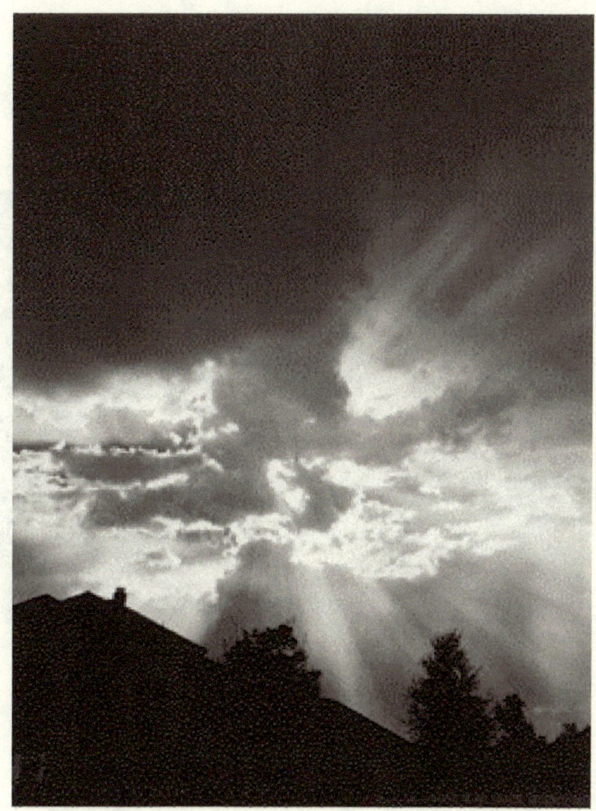

Lubbock, Texas

Hamilton, Ontario, Canada

Day 5 / 26 September

The Brook of Life

(It's a fantastic story in today's world!)

Like a thin blue strip line,
Saw it from the skies
Yearning for years,
Stumbled on it, too late!

Was it a mockery of fate,
a second chance to date?
Let sail as Ponce's mate,
Fill up your bucket to sate!

The raven wall shines with stars!
Bathe from Dionysus' earthen jars!
Lay on the cumulus to slumber!
To feel the brook of life's no-better?

Let pass the marching days!
Pose with the scorching rays!
Blow the misty dusts away!
Embrace the maiden as she lays!

Postscript:
Ponce De Leon once sailed to look for the fountain of youth.
Dionysus is the god of wine.

A Cast of My Hand

- A Brain Tumor Gone, a Young One,
- An Unexpected Path

How do I remember you, my child?
When storm river flowed on dry bed,
As dark shadows blurred by clouds,
And we step on unchartered mound?

How do we tell strangers about you?
With all the tales and woes as a bro?
Not the desperate Dad's wish to let go,
Too late, to take you away from this woe!

A widow, a widower, not for a dearest one!
Such is the law, yet Job fought this foe!
He knelt and prayed on the desert sand,
We smile as we carry a cast of your hand!

Day 6 / 27 September

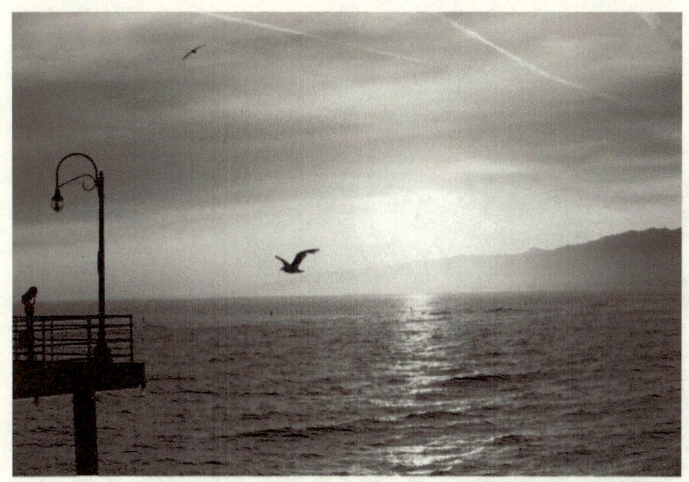

Balboa, California

Baronia / The Autumn of Dreams / 18

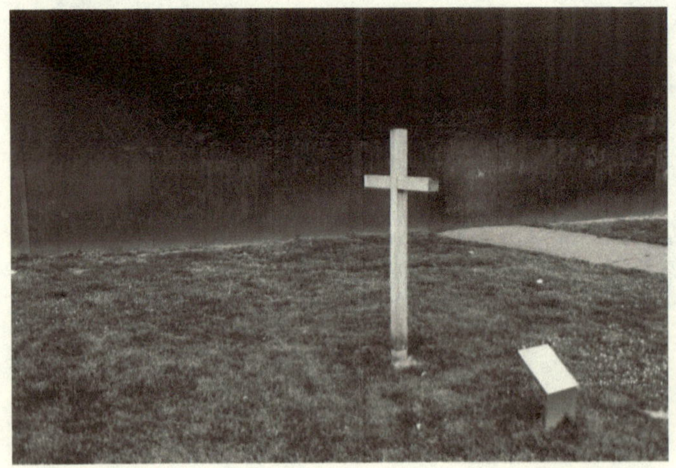

Berlin, Germany

Day 7 / 28 September

The Usual Prayer

I don't know how my world will be, once all of this is over.

I don't know how all the stuff that I started will end as I get my freedom.

I don't know how my children will face the future with their battered minds.

I don't know how all others will view what I've been through with all the hullabaloo.

I know for sure I'll do everything --

to heal my children so they can succeed

and be happy!

to seek my dream and hold tight my full point.

even I won't succeed, am sure I'll still be so happy trying with all my spirit to the end!

I'll pray so help me God!

The Fangs of Sleeplessness

Do you wait for a cloudless night to reach out for the stars?

Do you try to catch the sunrays with an open palm?

Do you dry the soil beneath you as the rain falls?

Why bother to shout to hear your echo of anguish?

Why lift the weight to unburden one's loneliness?

Why sing the joy of love when no one listens?

It is not by standing up that one sees the path!!

It is not by weaving on to distant past that sparks up the future!

To be joyful is to care for someone without bounds!

Day 8 / 29 September

Lubbock, Texas

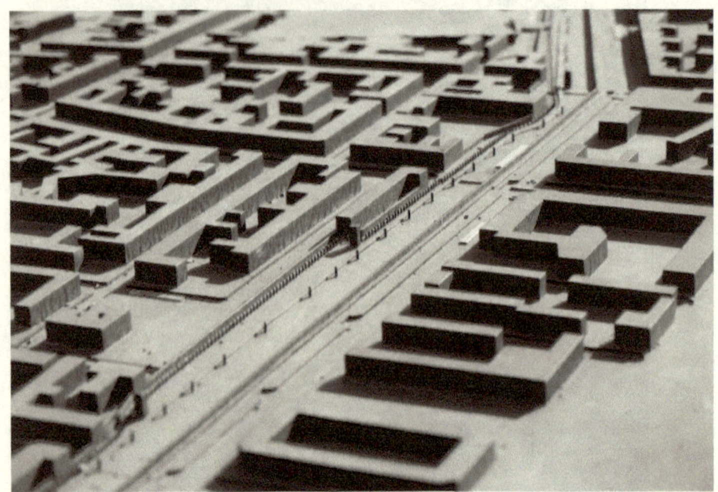

Berlin, Germany

Day 9 / 30 September

Soliloquy's Stampede

I dread the silence. I hate the unknown. I abhor the wicked.
I accepted this fate. I will endure the distress.
when pain is too pervasive, it dulls the senses.
I'll not wait for tomorrow, will keep this day to rest.
another day means to reset my nerves.
a new day is to brine wash my open wound.
I play the major role for this tale.
and if I wanted to act this part until the end,
I must carry the weight beyond Mt Calvary,
so I can be worthy of the last psalm,
it can be a tragedy where I can be freed forever;
a parable, where I can be a shadow as dark as the night.
satire, where I'll still be with no one but with His precious gifts.
a love story, as I lay down on a marked bench, my words echoed.
This was just after a mug of light miller blue...

A Family Haiku

A gal from Frisco
with her two lovely kiddos
chat with her, my aim!

let me hear your voice,
not to rush but to cherish
this day on forward.

//about your son//
a towering height
although higher than your mom
son's love much higher.

//about your daughter //
dearest lovely one
like your mom, daintier than Kate*
she's Brit, you, Venus!

//this time about your family//
the three of us here
world around us is complete?
let's add, a new one?

Day 10 / 01 October

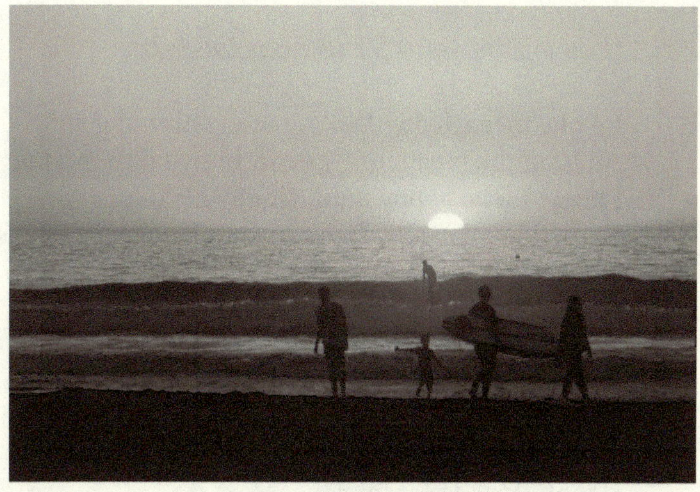

Manhattan Beach, California

The Other Sun of My Life

(Random thoughts for this special day)

I woke up each day looking at the morning sun,
As I felt the breath of fresh air blown thru my lungs.
I knew I'll be happy until the day is done.
Everything happens smoothly not by chance but as planned.
I know why each day am happy to see the sun,
With the bright future ahead it ensures that's fun!
All our lives, we're all grateful, me being her son,
The other sun of my life, our lives, she is my mom!

Happy Birthday, Mom.

We love y'all!

Day 11 / 02 October

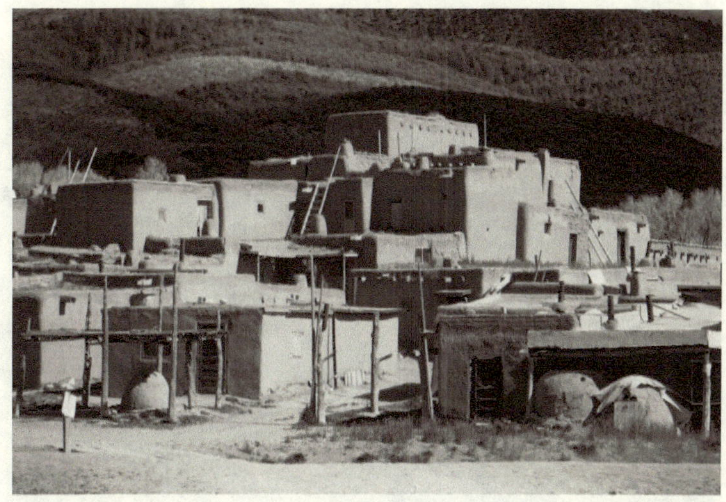

Taos, New Mexico

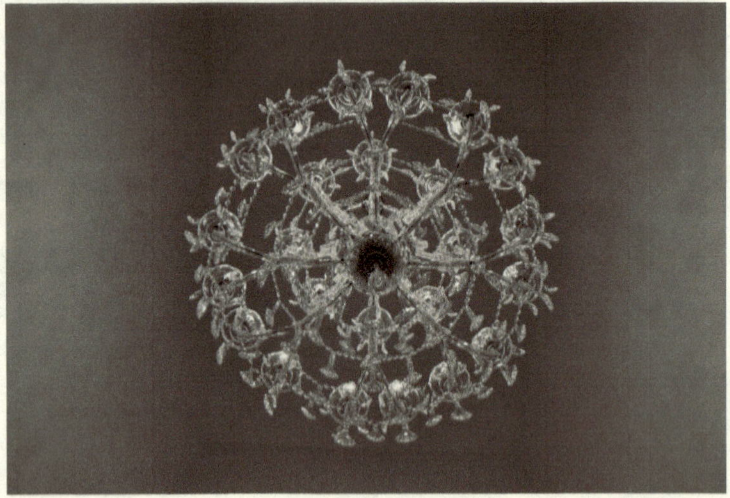

Hamilton, Ontario, Canada

Day 12 / 03 October

The Spark Wheel

The wheel of spark

Let's spin our wheel.

Each is with a different size.

Each groove is for what we want.

We spin it and we hope it will stop

At one common point, ours will meet.

The chance is simply infinitesimal.

Endless Sight

Each day, each night,

I look at your face,

brings smile, not sigh!

Move on, shy away,

dance, sing and play,

enjoy life and fly!

I'll stay around,

be still, hope abound,

I can see you from afar!

Day 13 / 04 October

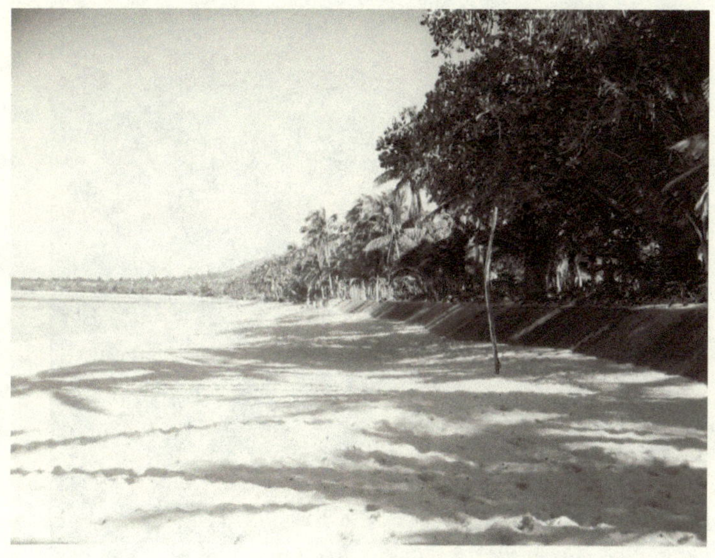

Pagudpud, Ilocos, Philippines

Baronia / The Autumn of Dreams / 32

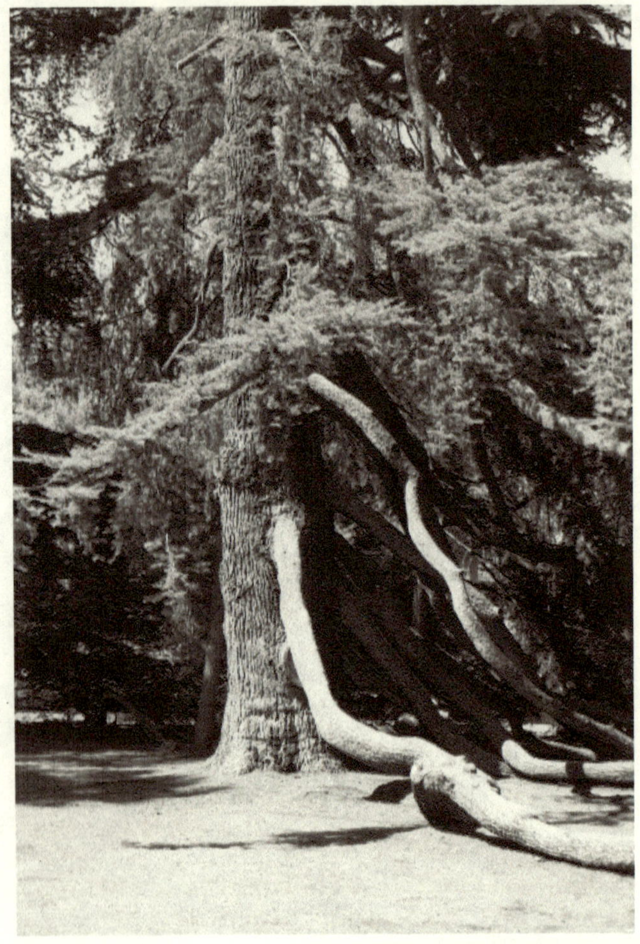

Pasadena, California

Day 14 / 05 October

A Unicorn and A Goddess

I see you as a goddess,

For I don't seek a goddess,

Instead, I pray for one.

I woo her over the heaven.

Dream about her as I close my eyes.

Never dare to even speak to her.

or look at her for longer time.

To fix my gaze will blur her images.

To listen, will flood my ears with joy of ecstasy,

and if I persist, will I no longer be a human?

But be a spirit who'll roam the universe in eternity?

The Last Box

One last box to tick.
I do care if I did,
today or in 2030.
easy but I can't,
not 'id' but respect!

not to linger,
not to reminisce,
not to ponder,
just to meet.

not for minutes,
not to repeat.
not to 'text'.
just for a sec!

glimpse meant a lot!
read a line.
smile and chuckle.
that's all in life!

Day 15 / 06 October

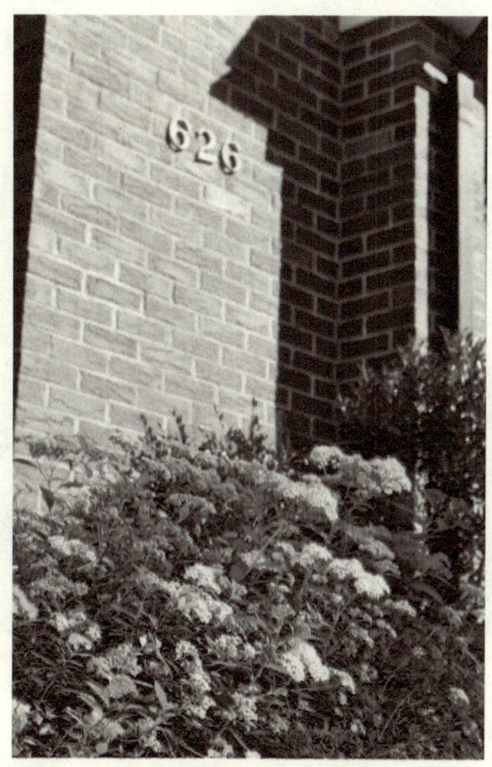

Webster Groves, St. Louis, Missouri

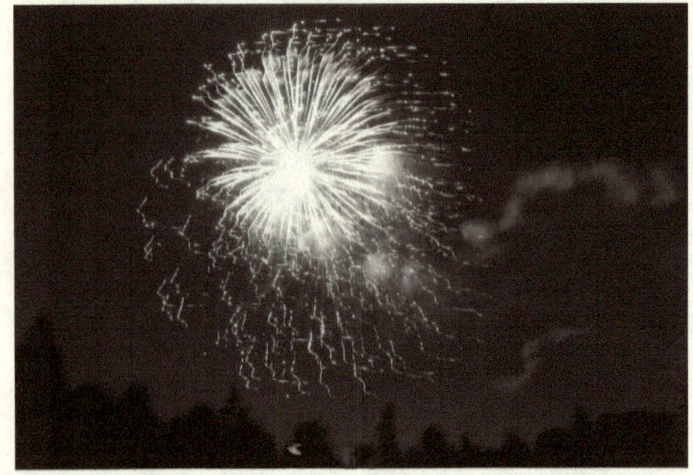

Toronto, Ontario, Canada

Day 16 / 07 October

The Online Galaxy

Am not sure, how long each one will wait till they stop and decide to move on to go offline and to meet.

am not even sure, if ever there will be an end while being online.

for I think, to look for the stars, one does not gaze and admire each one.

that single star may be part of a long existing group of constellations

one can't ask that star to leave and be part of one's life.

so look down and wonder, walk along the beach,

a different star pushed by the waves from the depth to the shores.

exposed to the sun and moon with each flash of tide.

wow, don't look up and try to reach that far!

just kneel down like a prayer, there's that star,

bare and naked, natural and unspoiled.

just waiting to be chosen and be held.

not too tight but gently.

now, just continue to walk and smile

till the end of time.

A Wish for Casper

Persistence is the antithesis of failure!

ghosting is so prevalent nowadays!

hope Casper ends this.

Day 17 / 08 October

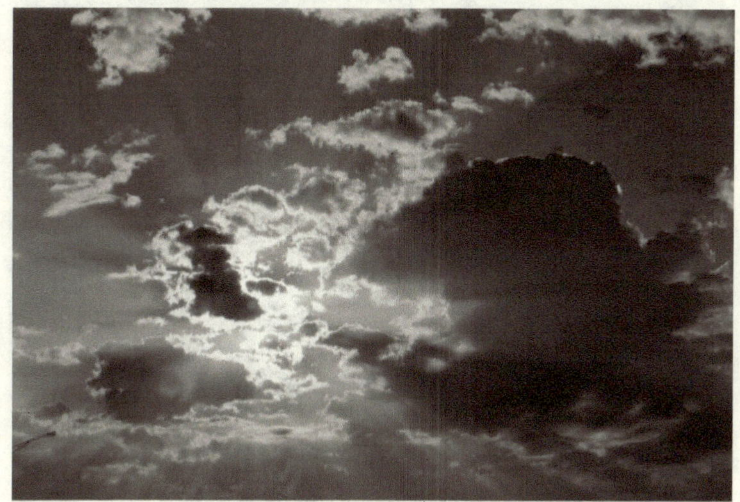

Lubbock, Texas

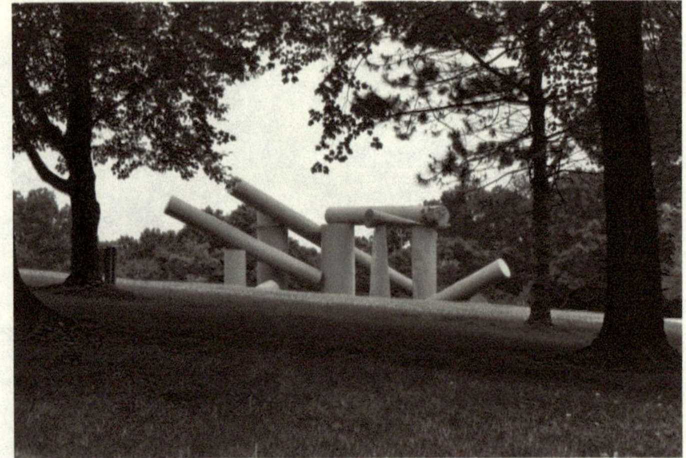

St. Louis, Missouri

Day 18 / 09 October

Time is on My Side

To rush an ebb tide.
a wind to brush aside.
a whisper to loud.

Why bother to look?
Lots of 'wish-me-luck'!
Geeks, Richie rich, hunks!
Yea, am an old doc!

Your beauty's quite odd.
Makes myself feels cold.
To aspire and be bold!
To walk down the road!

To wait for heaven's sake,
To be ghosted, that's fine!
Earth was flat for eons.
Am real and am true!

The ABC of Knowing

How do you measure the depth of the ocean?
As you fly thru the skies?
How do you feel the softness of the fur?
By blowing thru the air.
How do you tell the firmness of a rock?
As you whistle an aria?
How do you tell someone that she's the only one?

When you look from afar, her radiance fills your day
When you touch her skin, you can feel her soothing smile
When you listen to her words, her wisdom becomes yours!

Go share her the agony of your tears.
Kneel as your knees bend with ease
Let the echo of your laughter fill her dream
Write her the song that keeps on playing!

Life is a mystery.
Pain is evanescence.
Joy is extraordinary!
Love is certain!

Day 19 / 10 October

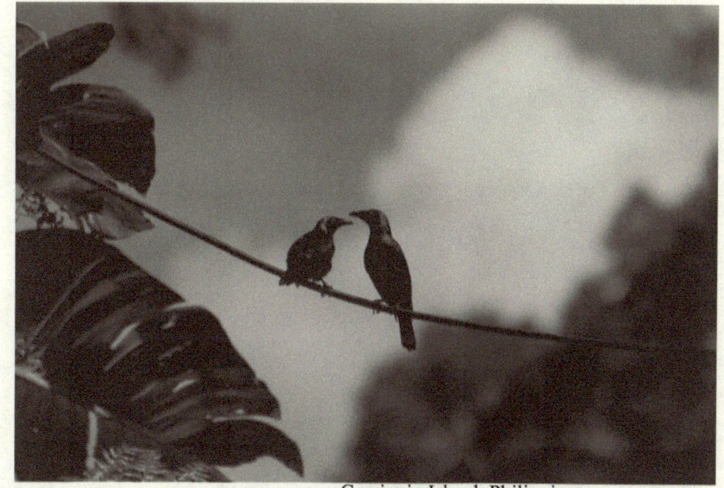

Camiguin Island, Philippines

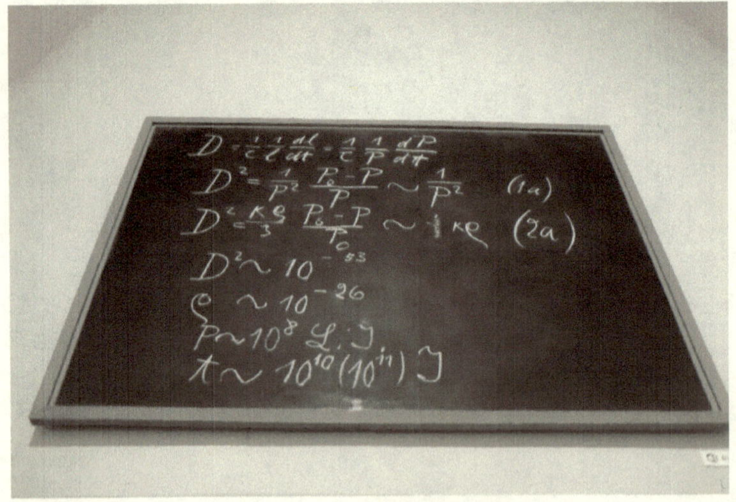

Oxford, United Kingdom

Day 20 / 11 October

Distance is Relative

Why do you marvel at the distant star on a moonless night?
Why do look afar when you hear a thunder?
Why do you dream to be someplace of peace?
and yet you ponder that distance bars you?

It's an unfair exchange between distance and with something that might end up timeless, boundless and maybe lots of laughter.

It's not about me solely, it's about a man that you might meet not only with a big spark but you-know-what and then you realized that he is not from your place but from…

Krypton, and he's Clark Kent! LOL

For the Patriotic Woman

I Can Wait

Persistence is the antithesis of failure

Failure thrives among retreaters.

Retreat is the panacea for hopeless creatures

Hopelessness is the cocaine for depression.

Depression breeds 'unjoyfulness'.

Day 21 / 12 October

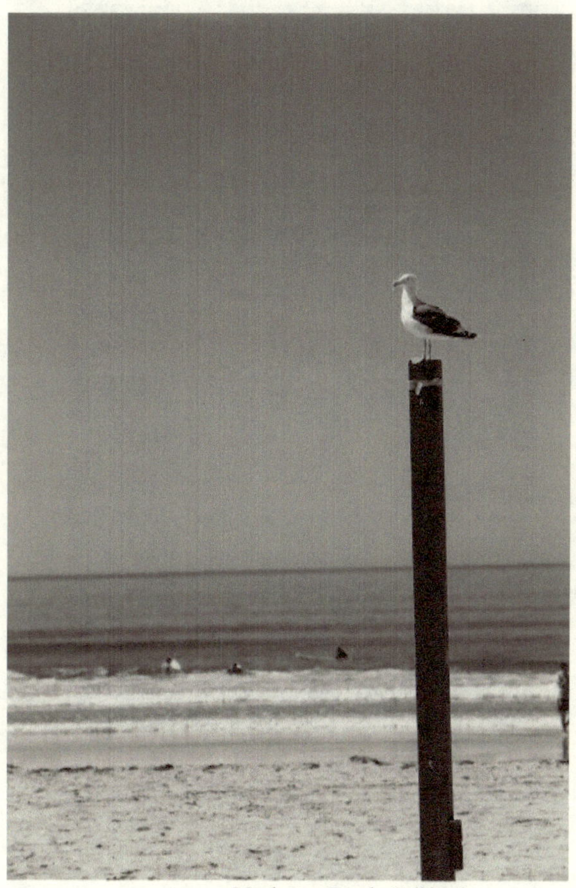

Manhattan Beach, California

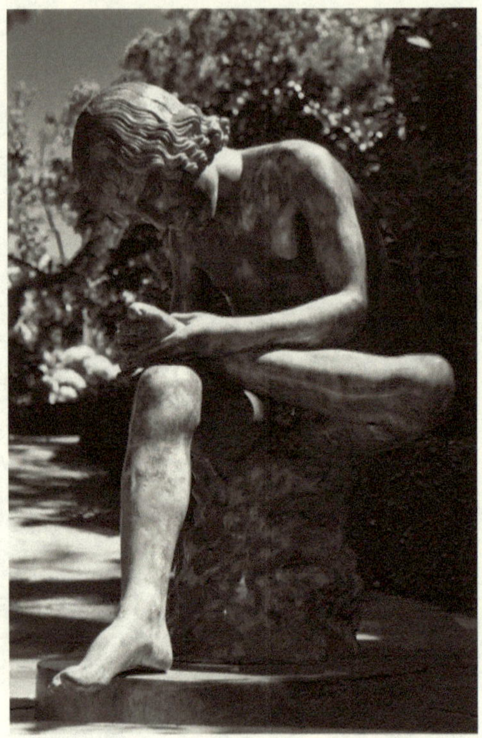

Hearst Castle, California

Day 22 / 13 October

Dearest Angela

I woke up this morning thinking about your mom. Looking back last night with all of you at her bedside was quite a sight. There's a lot of love around her! That alone oftentimes will make a big difference! For sure, someone up there sees all of that. Even with our great and vast knowledge, there are things we won't comprehend wholly! Events that happen may not be in conformity with what we all wanted.

Let me share y'all this random thought …

Why do things happen as they should not be?
When it should be much easier where the sun should be?
At daytime, we look east then follow it to the west."
When life starts at birth
and moves on like a breeze?
Why can't we all be happy
as events unfold?
With all the love and prayers we behold?
Do we understand about
Adam and Eve's fault?
Do we feel the joy of life
after a nine month-fold?
Thc humanity in us falters,
we can't understand,
even saints do!
Such is the plan, a great plan, only He knows!"

God bless and have a nice day for y'all!

The Dawn of Dating

**Dawn is her real name, a teacher and a mother of two.*

The beauty at once glance

truly a pic which launches ships

dunno how to stop typing

to express one's awe and appreciation

maybe another time, someday

another random thought, nice to share!

have a good evening, D.

Day 23 / 14 October

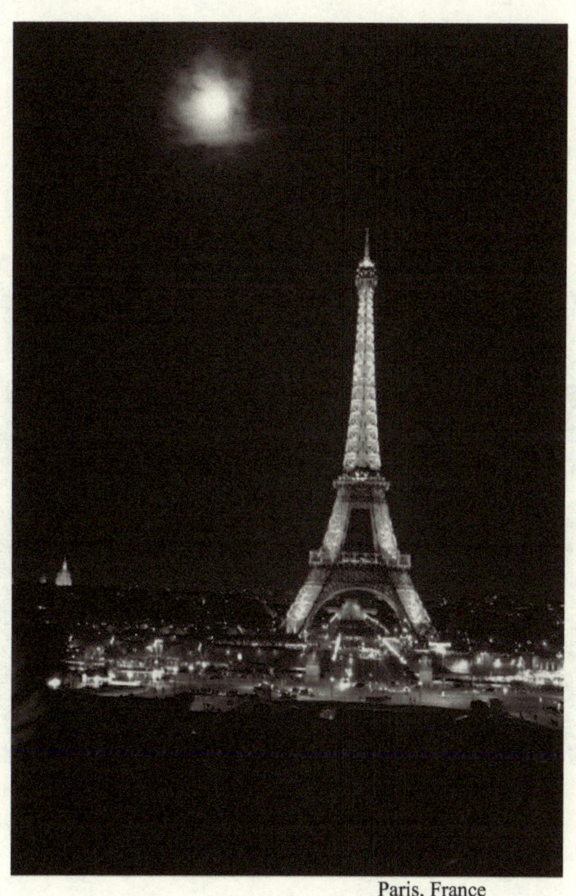

Paris, France

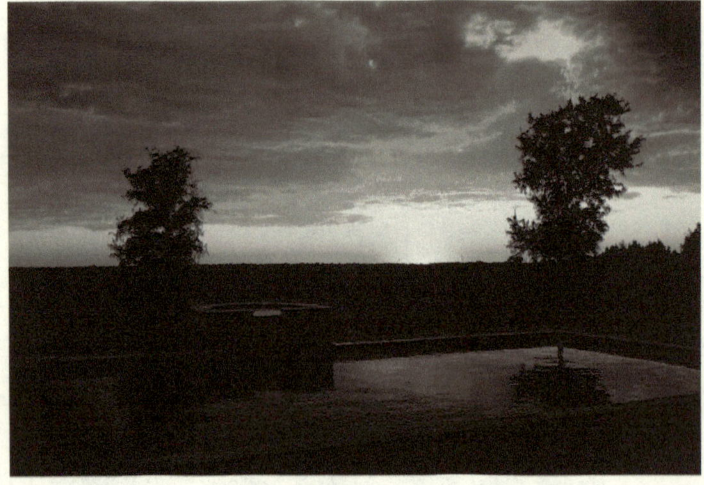

Lubbock, Texas

Day 24 / 15 October

Life is a Mirage

What do y'all see when I smile?
Did y'all see the dry tears I shed?
What do y'all feel when I cry?
Did y'all hear the bruit on my ear?
What do y'all read with my mac?
Did y'all sense the silence of the keys?

Do you seek happiness at your loved ones' misery?
Do you find joy with their sorrow?
Do you end today with a better tomorrow?
Do you wish for the stars at day?
Do you look for someone with a blind eye?
Do you dare so others may care?

Always choose good over evil.
What may be obvious may not be real.
To love everyone leaves a spark.
To be scorned bares no mark.
Walk uphill with righteousness.
To stumble, to stand with zest!

Etre Mere

I will never know how to bear a babe for 9 moons,
I'll be too eager to hear the first breath of one's cries!
Each day, each week, each month, I'll tag each quiver!
And I'll build one's place in our hearts on that great day!

Have you seen a mom as she nurtures her young,
As she does multiple tasks as heaven can only see?
How about the tears of joy and laughter for every baby's step?
With the tireless efforts to keep one's well in sickness and in health?

Day 25 / 16 October

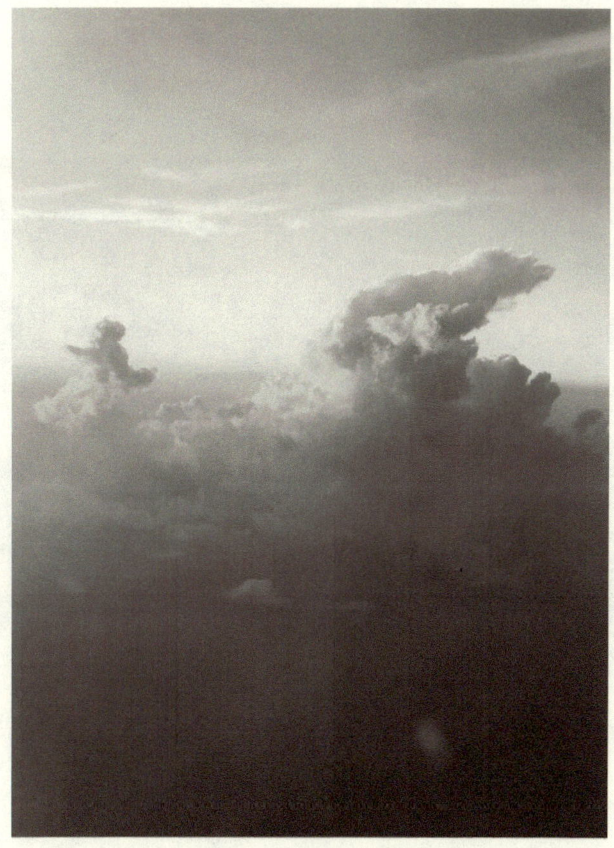

Lubbock, Texas

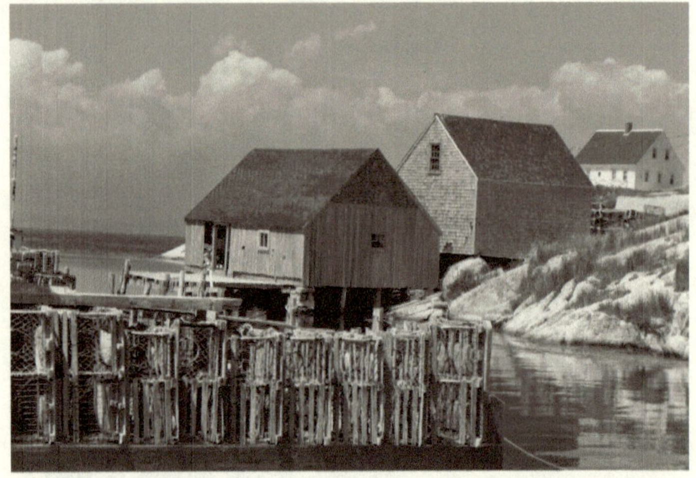

Halifax, Nova Scotia, Canada

Day 26 / 17 October

To Capture Beauty

Now, that my thoughts are poked
with my fingers jumping from keys
to digitize those peaks and troughs
as they travel thru the hippocampi
to capture beauty to eternity
is as easy as typing the right keys!
have a good night again, D.

A Perfect Date v.1

You see me as I am.
I look at you as you are.
we both see eye to eye.
both of us with zero to hide,
everything floats in air,
as we laugh, we enjoy.
then we say goodbye
and ask ourselves, what now?
and in unison, we both say,
we'll do it again, next time!

Day 27 / 18 October

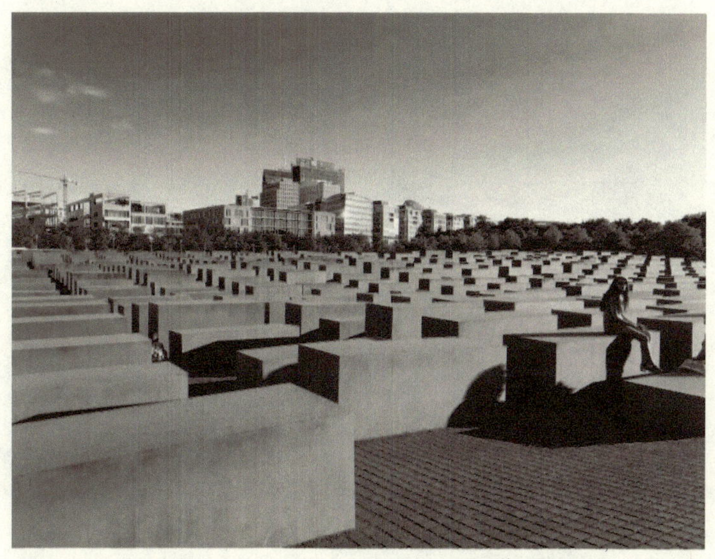

Berlin, Germany

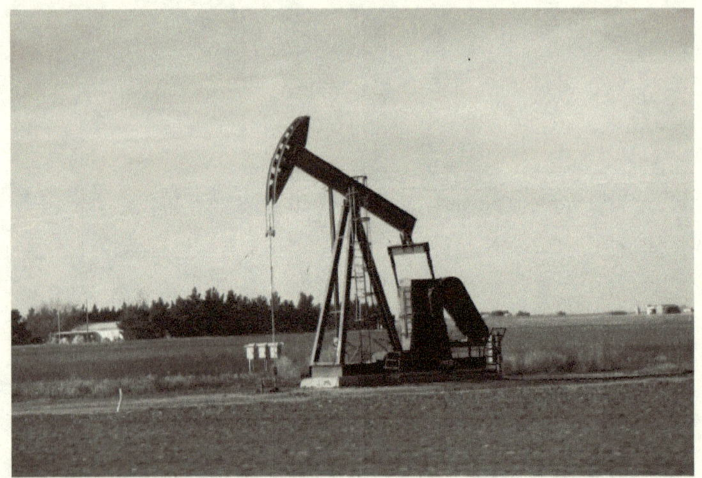

Abilene, Texas

Day 28 / 19 October

A Perfect Match v.1

I thought perfection exists in heaven,
for humans are made as 'replicants'.
we try to be exactly as the One!
with frailties and being half blind,
until we both meet at the middle,
sometimes at your end and mine.
perfection will nowhere to be found.

Lea

It is this smile that all men will look for.

It is this smile which exudes beauty sans par

It is this smile that no one can put asunder

It is this smile that I'll be content with eyes barred

It is this smile that I'll look for even from afar!

Day 29 / 20 October

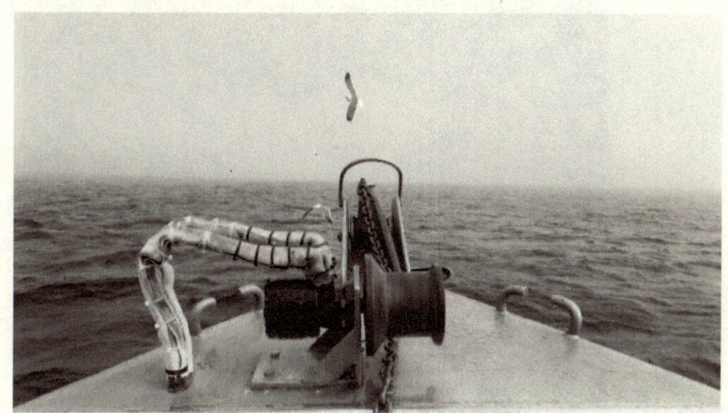

Dana Point, California

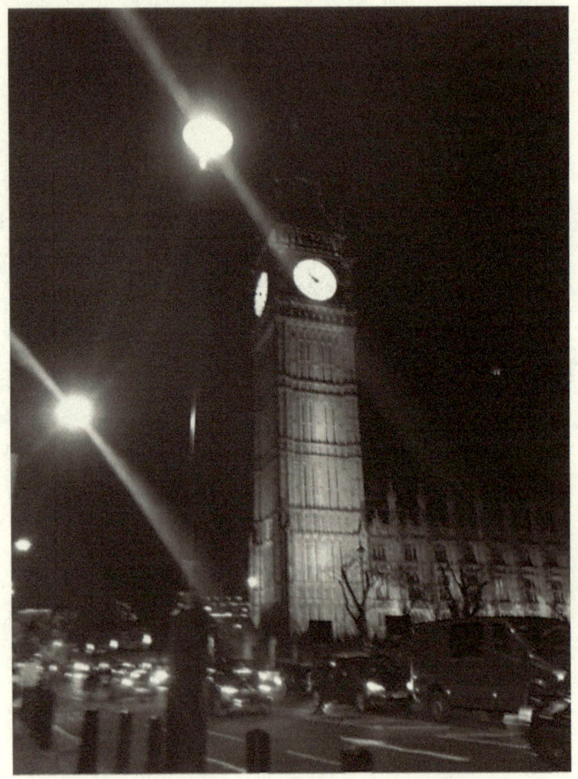

London, United Kingdom

Day 30 / 21 October

A Perfect Match v.2

Will I look up at the sun when you cry
To let my own tears dry up as I cuddle you in my arms?
Will I say no to things I love
To let most of the things you care we both hug?
Will I laugh when you make fun
To let me float in your dream within the clouds?

Or

would you rather enjoy the songs we haven't heard?
Dine with our hands with food we haven't tasted?
Dance with the waves with each moon's cycle?
Sway with each blade of grass at the wake of the sun?

Or

Just be us altogether no matter what.
You are you.
I am I.

Together, let's live our lives,
once separate lives as ONE!

A Smile

Is this the smile that shines a moonless night?

Is this the smile that melts the ice on eaves?

Is this the smile that warms one's bare hands

Is this the smile that calms a baby's cry?

Is this the smile that God made to make peace?

I know this smile led me typed these keys

I know this smile made me dream of heaven.

I know this smile will make me rest for tonight.

Have a wonderful evening, LTL

Day 31 / 22 October

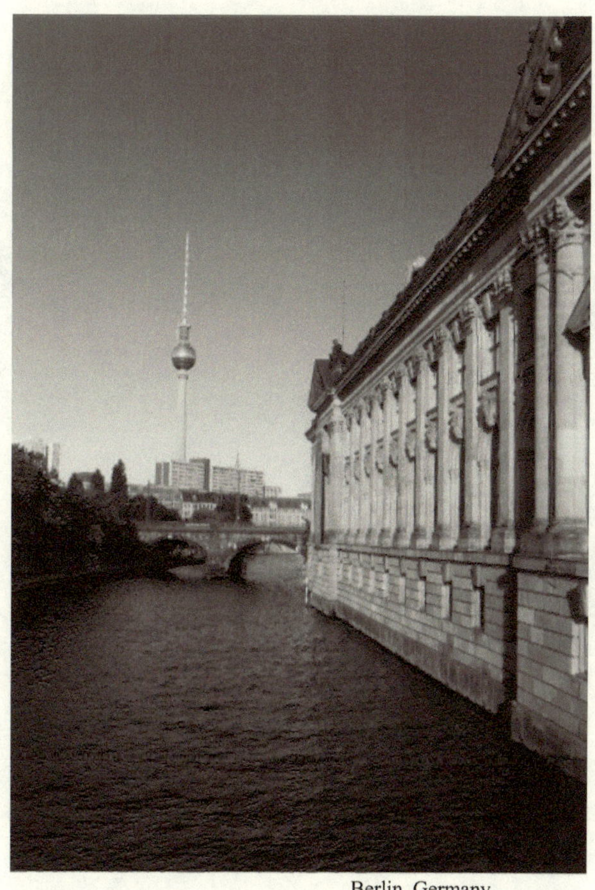

Berlin, Germany

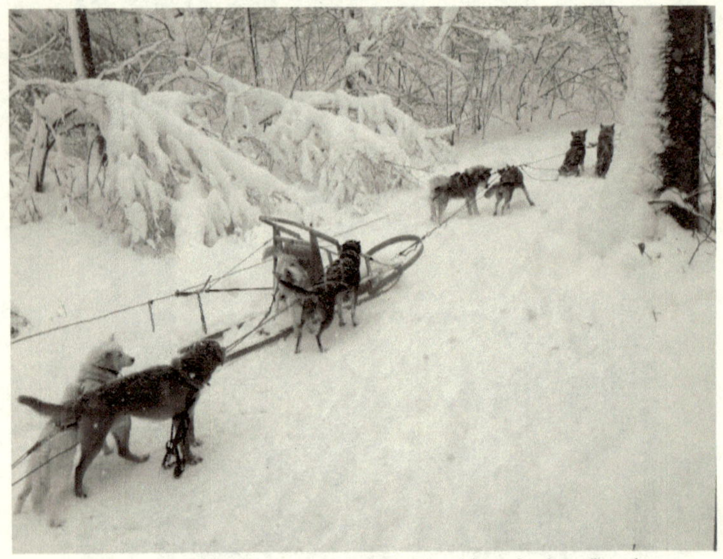

Mt. Tremblant, Quebec, Canada

Day 32 / 23 October

An Irony of Laughter (LTL)

What do you see with a flash of lightning?
What do you hear with the sound of the drums?
It is easy to see the light and hear the boom,
Not when one's mind is nowhere on focus!

Flip open the Mac-air and type the keys.
Scroll with your fingers and look up and down.
Did 'LTL' log in and ask for a chat?
Did I miss it and now she's forever gone?

Oh, this digital world where we just met.
I didn't even glance at her smile before she was gone.
Those smiles glued to my brain for life and even in my dreams.
I'll stay awake for long.
I wait until I see,
'LTL' pops up again on the screen.

Till death of my computer
or my battery runs out and I need to plug in.

It's good to see you again, Lea.

To Express One's Awe and Appreciation

Maybe another time, someday
another random thought, nice to share
have a good evening, Dawn.
my apologies
the image that I often see
as I flip open my mac air enough for someone to say
let me lie and rest for the day I've seen an angel today
and I still yet long for heaven
have a good night, again. Dawn. :)
now, that my thoughts are poked
with my fingers jumping from keys
to disguise those peaks and troughs
as they travel thru the hippocampi
to capture beauty to eternity
is as easy as typing the right keys!
have a good night again, Dawn

Day 33 / 24 October

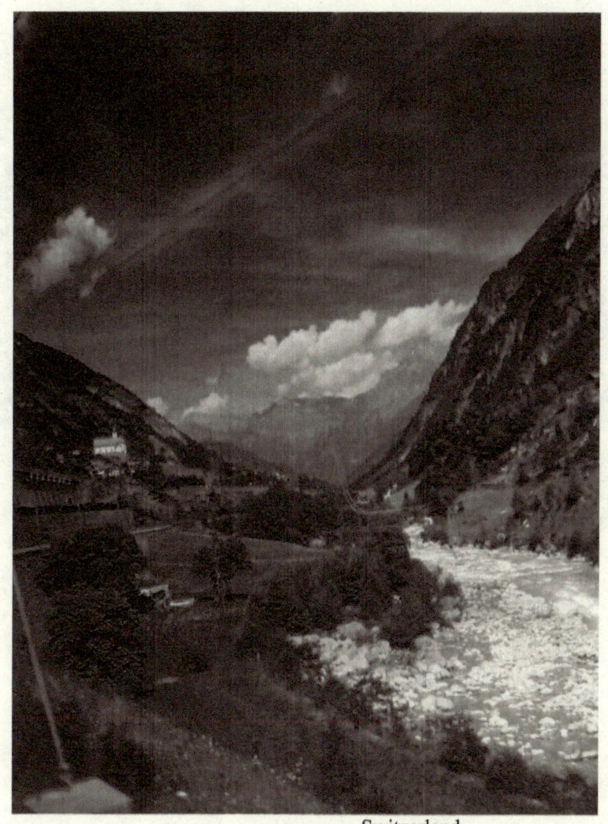

Switzerland

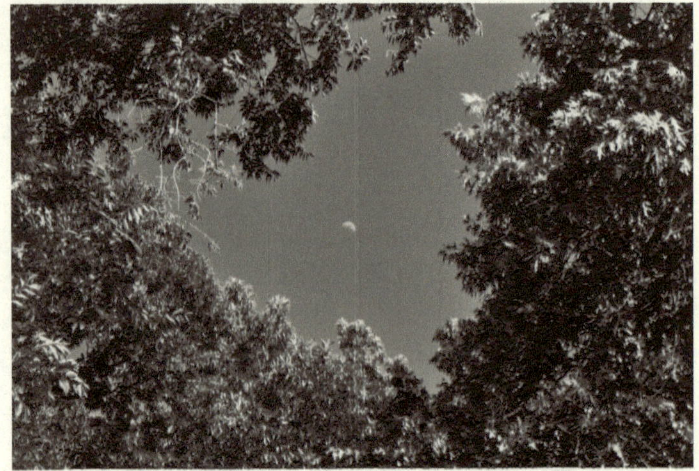

St. Louis, Missouri

Day 34 / 25 October

A Perfect Date FINAL VERSION

I think this is the closest I can think of

'Love Made in Heaven - A Dream Forever', the book just

published

//you gave me a chance,

for there's the 'x,' the 'IT,' the 'magic.'
and whatever we decide to do,
Time ceases to exist! //

A Perfect Date, Second Version :)

Perfection does not come easily,

After a glimpse of your pic, maybe just one or many,
Read your profile and decided to click 'add' or 'wink.'
By chance, you responded after a thousand guys did the same.
Pictures and writings are just windows to peep in.
In the end, meeting someone for a casual chat may add.
But there's the 'X,' the 'IT,' the magic; you don't know what!
Those who had once and ended up here, we knew what's best!
A lot of them, difficult to find, if she's there, we'll find each other!
It maybe with a glass of wine, candle-lit dinner, a movie to watch ·
Sports live or TV, a concert in the park, a stroll along the beach,
A game of pool, a bike ride, or just together looking up the stars,
Regardless, the feeling of being one and laughter, that's the one!

Day 35 / 26 October

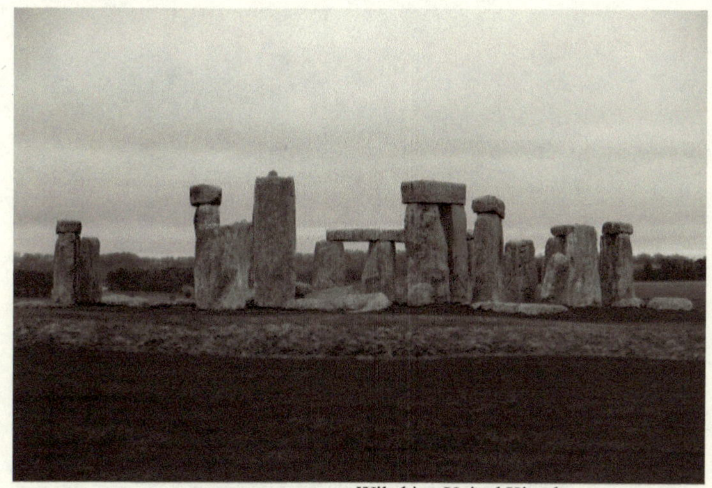

Wiltshire, United Kingdom

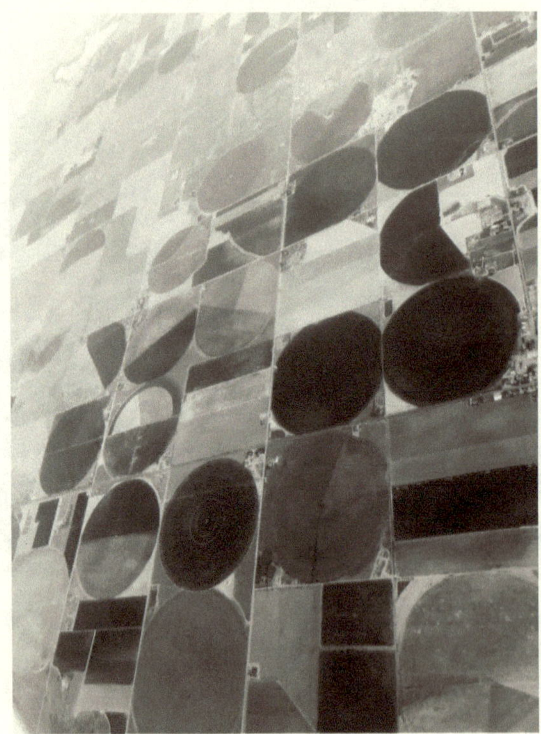

Lubbock, Texas

Day 36 / 27 October

Distance is Relative v.2

Diamonds are not created in days or weeks

in moonless night, a flicker of light from afar may be enough to guide one's path

thunder so distant can be heard on a silent night

a whisper of hope or expression of love is a sweet music among the noisy crowd

that's why distance is nonsense but a relative barrier

created by our imagination but not by those who think

that love made in heaven can be possible on earth after all

LOL

those are my random thoughts for you Kelly

A Woman of My Dream

As I logged online with my mac to get a glimpse of what's in it

A day to day wish of something maybe a spark, a tiny interest

but never a dream of my life behold, t'was not the same

as I saw your face, and read your profile

I knew, I found at last the woman of my dream

not sure it will be true at her end or her wish

just being a friend and knowing her

meeting her will be enough

like a lost person on a moonless night

struggling to see the path with the single star even afar

a sigh of contentment that life can be meaningful

any day, any time with a stroke of faith

with opening my mac at that instance

my life would change I think for I found

a friend...a woman of my dream.

Day 37 / 28 October

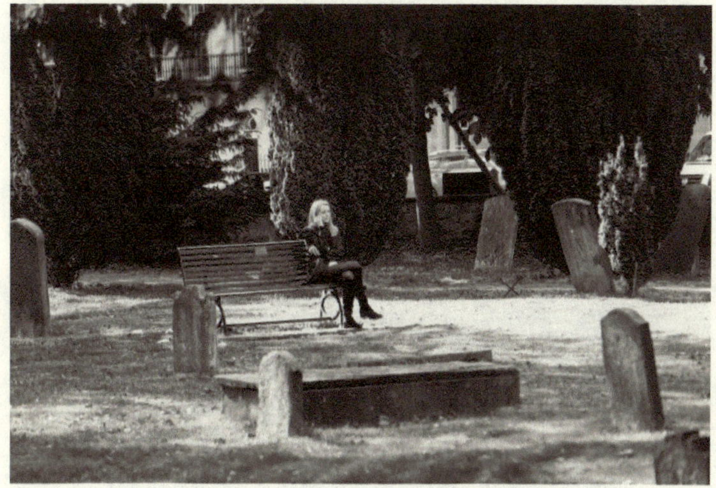

Oxford, United Kingdom

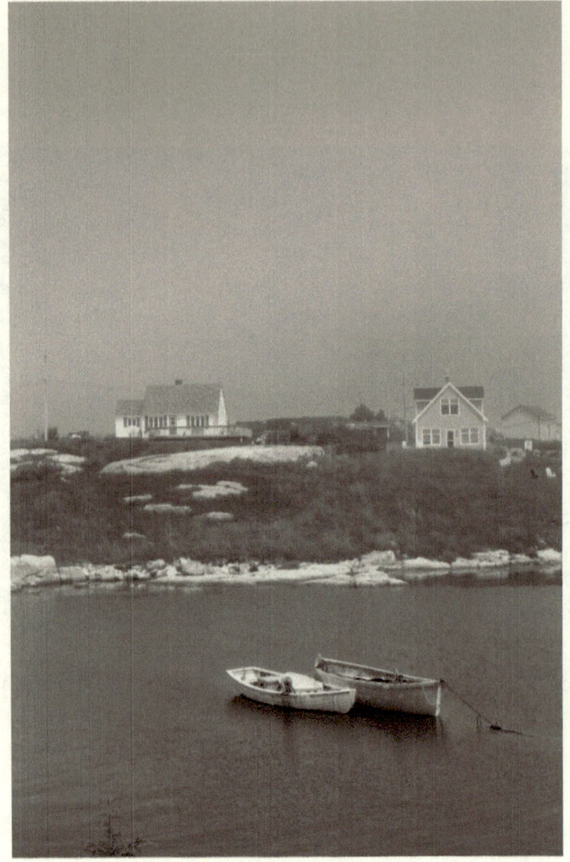

Halifax, Nova Scotia, Canada

Day 38 / 29 October

I See Beauty

I see beauty with the
scar of mastectomy,
It taught me the strength
to face one's mortality,
and the pain of healing!

I see beauty with
all the bodily curves
They were brought up
by stressful years as
I live my fruitful life
I see beauty with grey
hair and baldy scalps.
It reminded me the bitter
taste of chemo and the
wonderful looks of my oldies.

I see beauty in ALL
memories of my youth.
I see my friends, ne'er old
to hug them tightly as I
whisper, "I love y'all
and thanks so much
for just being here!

A Dozen Roses

A dozen roses,
A hundred grins,
A thousand laughs,
And a single bow!
Hope this brings you joy!
You've been working
So hard these days...
Smile, you're on God's sight!
Thanks :)

Day 39 / 30 October

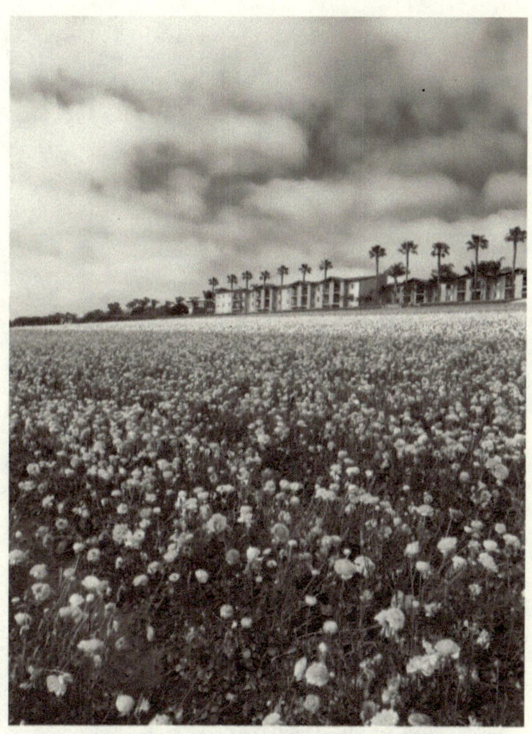

San Diego, California

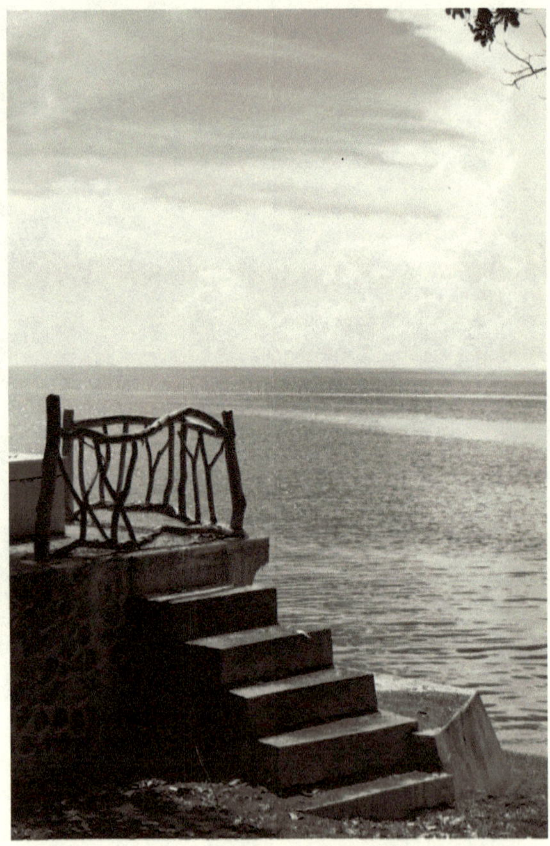

Camiguin Island, Philippines

Day 40 / 31 October

"Live Each Day to its Fullest"

What does survival rates mean to me?
is it a game of chance, one grim stat to be?
that out of so many, I might be lucky?

when will the world end, will it be before me?
when will I see the light last, as I close my eyes?
when will you shed tears, when it rains to blend?

remember me for those good memories!
forgive me for all my shortcomings!
stop loving me but love those I love most.

I won't feel the warmth of your touch!
I won't hear the sounds of your whisper!
I won't see the radiance of your smile!

I'm leaving with much joy!
my contentment I truly enjoy!
all of these from you and from all!!

I thank you, everyone and God.
my life I spent is (was) as meaningful as this –
BE happy, live each day to its fullest.
(my dearest lady with a big C!)

Tears of My Heart

(My apologies if I invoke sadness with this random thoughts)

Vivid memories in white,
Charts and urinals at hand,
Were those steth or hammer?
Taste of fluid where babies swam.

The walk of 'fully' or with 'AP',
As we watched from OB tower.
Code 64 meant q15 till sunrise,
As we grabbed meals in plastic packs.
"Who's on deck?", the dreaded line.

Let's wait for Limay, might be matched!
Who's the queen of beauty?
The champions at the court?

Writings on our shirts,
As we soaked ourselves with water?
AA, JB, GD, ED and AB, y'all part of these!
Your memories, our tears from our hearts!

Day 41 / 01 November

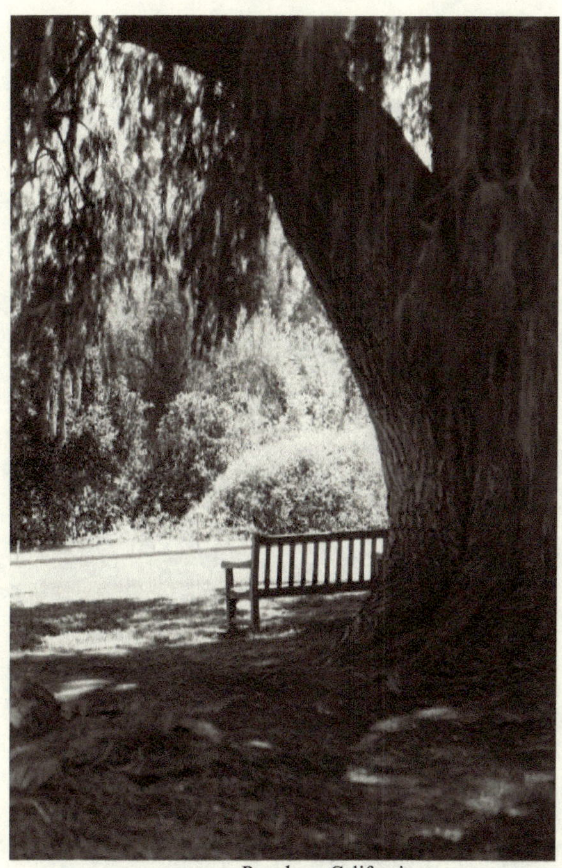

Pasadena, California

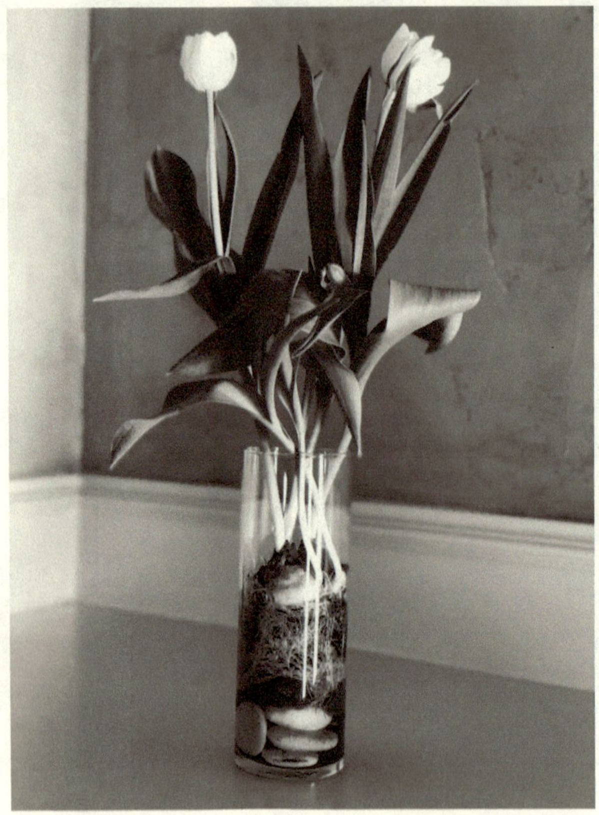

Lubbock, Texas

Day 42 / 02 November

"She"

Can I ever forget someone
with a great smile?
As I fumble with words and
she fills me in just fine.
Never did I encounter such a genuine
person, a caring mom!
Despite our differences,
she helps me every time.
At peace with her Christian values,
I am sway to a second chance.
Charming, sociable, firm, witty and
tirelessly enduring.
Every second that I have, I hope it's
with her for a joy of my being!

We Are A Different Breed

From the Games of Thrones,
The Joffrey's treat us as wildlings!
We are no kings or queens while
White stalkers and night kings abound!

The reality is we care no less for
Clients and relatives treat us highly!
Most colleagues envy our camaraderie!
We are UENSAA plus, the other world's kingdom!

In our sleep, we split Sylvian to see limen,
We stroll along the fibers of treitz
Gracefully, we align the axes of the spine
And join the minute vessels of PICA!

In our wakefulness, numbers and diet come easy!
42ks, 180km, 3.6; we are today's SEALs!
Sea, Air and Land, no carbs, we conquer!
At the end, we also do Neurosurgery!

Day 43 / 03 November

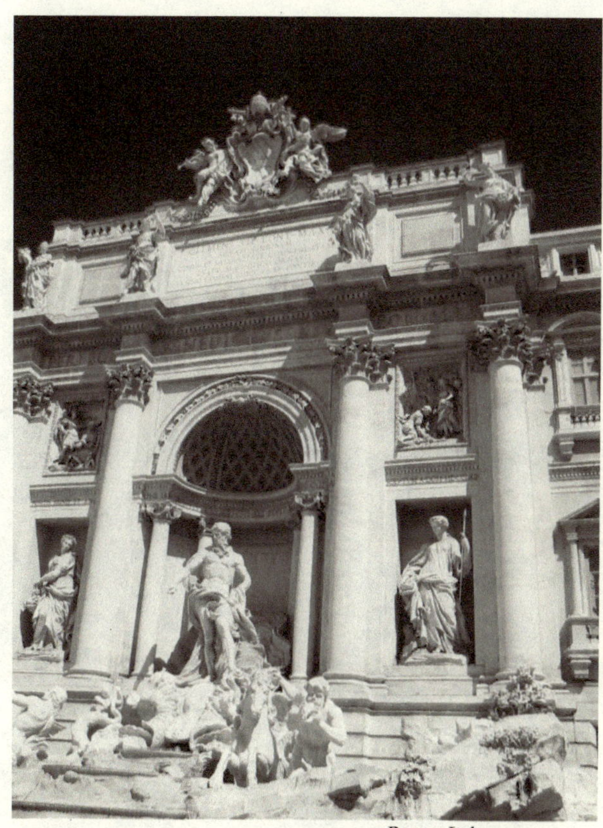

Rome, Italy

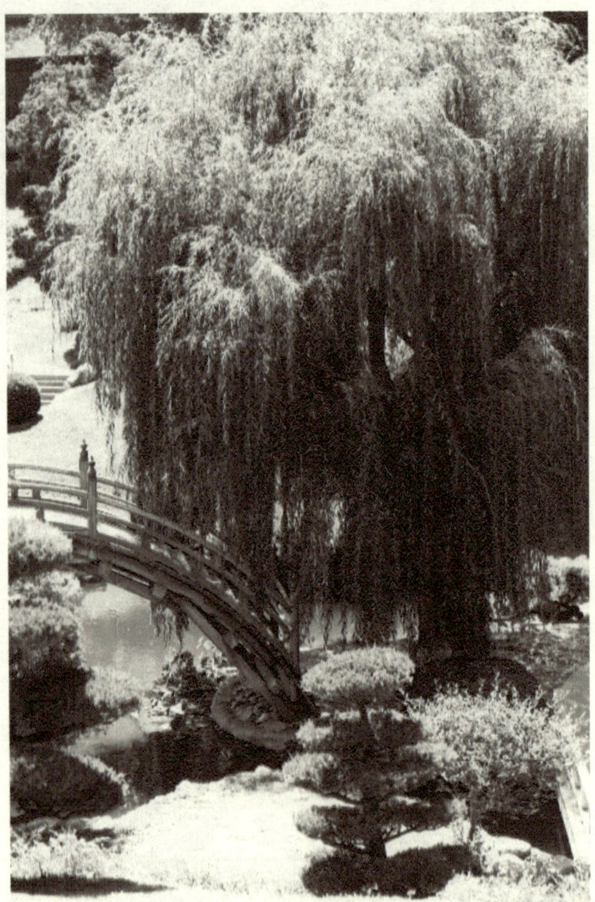

Pasadena, California

Day 44 / 04 November

Old Friends Last Forever

Years past with textured lines,
Smiles with wide-grinned jaws,
Voices maybe with tattered words,
Doubly-layered familiar gazes,

Memories of youth, happy ones,
Genuine laughter now abounds,
Remember those not with us,
Still, old friends last forever!

To Un-Friend is Divine

Go and glance at the inbox folder,
See the unread messages by the number,
Not much to really expect but to grin,
For it's quite just easy to 'un-friend!'

Each day is quite a long wait.
For it's another day to paint,
Perhaps let me change the tint,
From a dark hue to a sunlit!

Why frown if it's what it is?
Why be unhappy if it could be?
Flip the card to the other side,
Think of an ace to be a 'flush!'

From a poker game to darts,
Throw those tiny arrows hard.
For every bull's eye that I hit,
Let it burst my frustration to air!

And when my arms got tired,
Let me raise them up high,
And let me grab that magic bar
And turn myself upside down.
The best way to cope and win,
As you looked up at the Heaven,
Then like tossing a coin in Trevi's well,
Heaven is at your feet for a cotillion!

Day 45 / 05 November

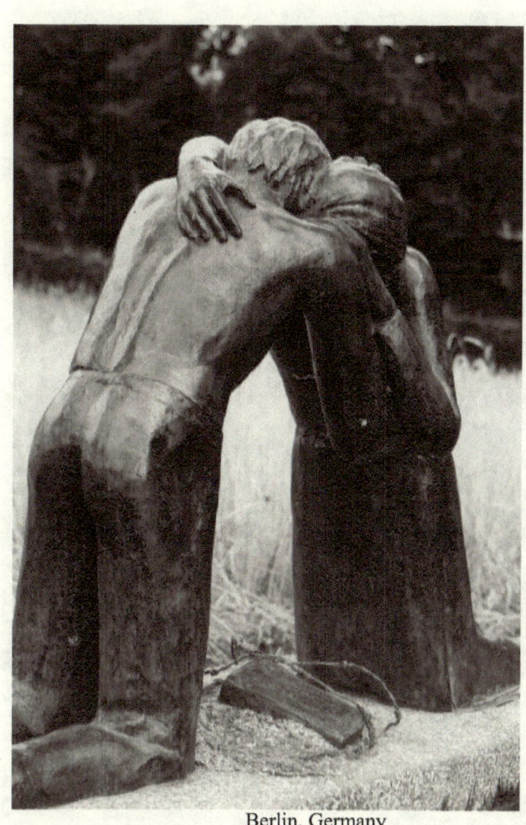

Berlin, Germany

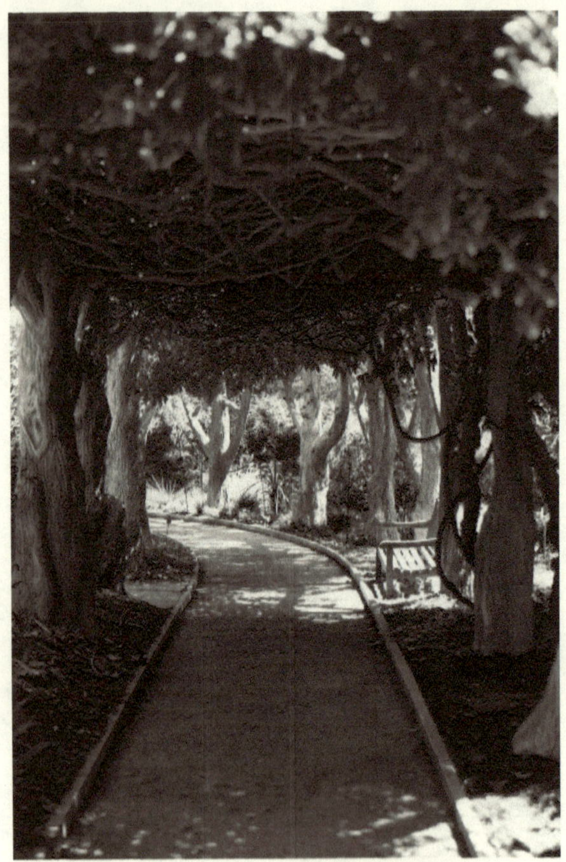

Pasadena, California

Day 46 / 06 November

Being Human

Path to greatness
I ventured to seek!
An endless toil with
flipping pages and
colored pens.
Lived with sines,
Slept with chems.
Wanted to build chip
to move non-man,
I moved masses to act!

Will it be white coat
Or white iron collar?
With Hollywood stars
or with usual locals?
Service to God or man?

UP, UST, St Louis, UE?
Or even Johns Hopkins!
Just above the line,
That's what mattered,
Scribbled form as proof!

To serve humanity!
To heed Hippocrates!
To see everyone
As He sees us!
Be a UERM MD, be human!

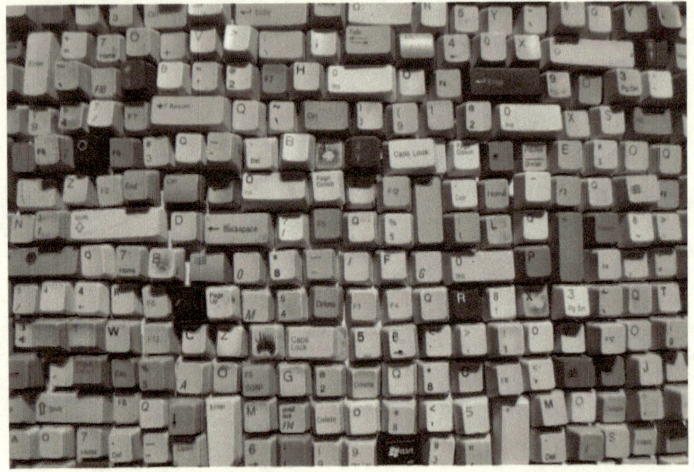

St. Louis, Missouri

Day 47 / 07 November

Beauty in the Beast!

How I looked with awe
The beauty we all bow to!
The daily sound of tick and tack,
Worked marvels with our lives!

Again, I tried, It went through,
My heart and mind molded into one!
Ones and zeroes rushed thru shades,
My eyes glimmered with hope!

Alas, to meet someone at the dark,
Not knowing, which ones to hold,
I guess, don't hurt oneself again,
Beware, there's beauty in the beast!

The 'Dee' is Cast

I walked a mile
here and there,
Not knowing
Where I would go!
Uncertain
of what to find!

On the ground,
I stumbled,
Fell on a rock!
I stood up
And polished it
To my great desire!

again, I continued,
Carried the load
Until the end.
Had realized,
T'was not a rock,
Not of anything
I found before!

With a confused mind
Asked men around,
Women, they scorned!
Just let go
And live your life
Just like before,
For the Dee is cast!

Day 48 / 08 November

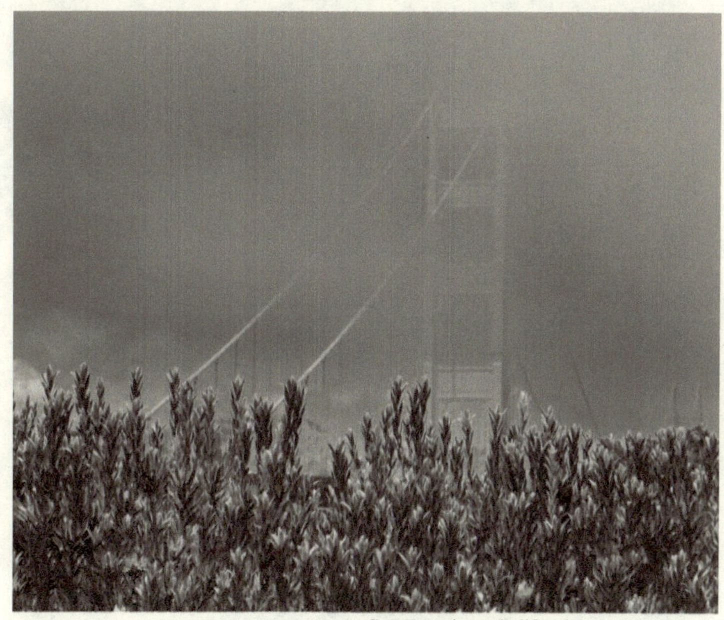

San Francisco, California

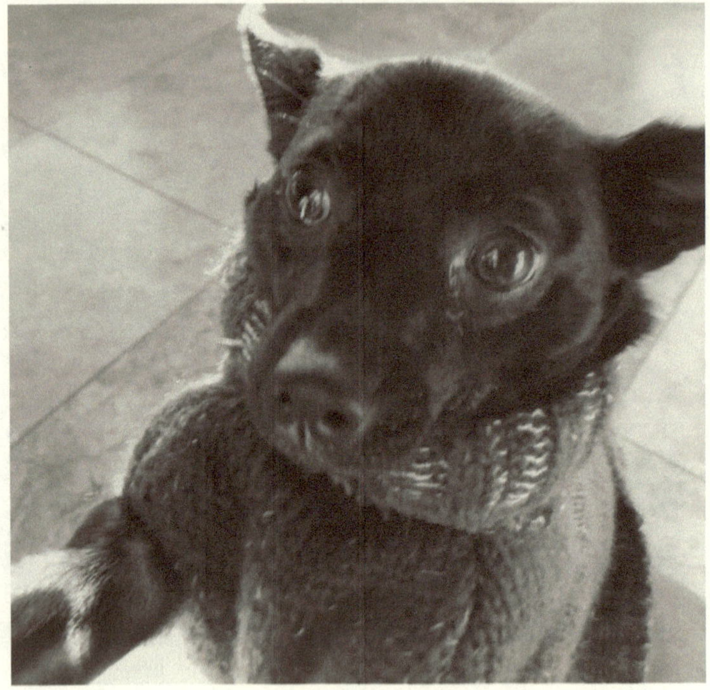

Lubbock, Texas

Day 49 / 09 November

Michael

He circles around

He jumps around

He looks at you

Each time all the time!

'A Recurring Tale'

Each day, each night, a painful one.
To wake up each time with an angst.
Life is cruel, to live life in a barren land.
To stare blankly, to stumble to dry!

Like a tumbleweed tossed by the wind,
Lacking roots, its Houston in the blind
Looking through the glass with a prism,
A kaleidoscope with a filter in chasm!

To set the stage so others may see.
A hackneyed story, maybe a mockery?
With the genuine care given and done.
Expected nothing but a joy to come!

From the first one at young at heart,
Wrote love letters and folded in style.
Two teener years later, texts by mobile,
Unread, maybe junked or shammed!

Smile, consider it's a luck, like an OREO,
Many may still like the brownies wall on
A sweet center always attracts minions,
As the 'Despicable One', be happy in eons!

Day 50 / 10 November

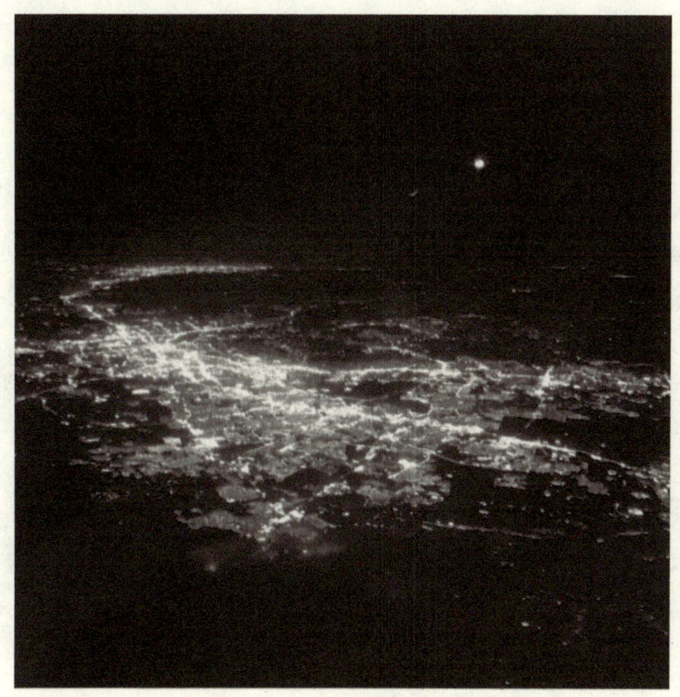

Lubbock, Texas

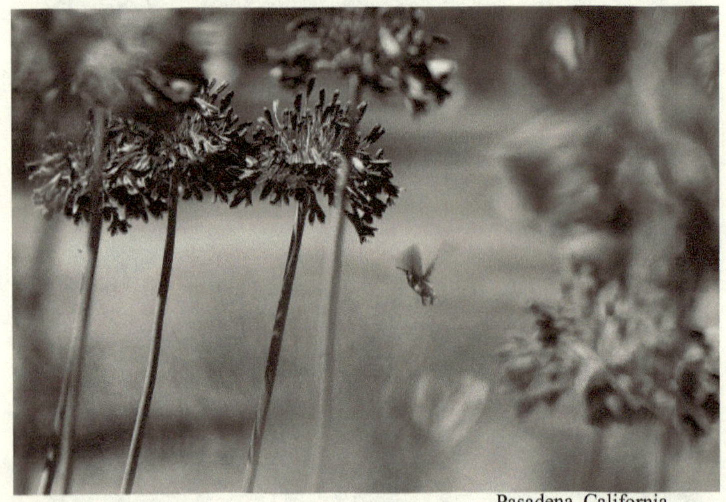

Pasadena, California

Day 51 / 11 November

The Greatest Talent of All

My random thoughts as I woke up @ HHGI Burbank and read thru those nice and marvelous missed texts when I was asleep. :) tried to post but failed, good thing, revised each time until its FULL :)

I wonder how I can bow the strings with smoothness,
I hold my breath as the heavenly piece is strummed with rhythm
I look with awe how the fingers crawl in frets along its neck!
I jump with glee with each score and bell in the field or at covered grounds!
I tap with my bare feet as I feel the gyrating hips,
I am full of positivity with silence and stillness of meditation,
I gasp with marvel when keys exude the voices of the angels,
I float in air when breaths of wind blow from whispers and thunder of arias,
I feel mute when the sounds of trumpet and sax permeate the air!
I cry with joy with each stroke of watercolors, oil and charcoal!
I stand up with buckled knees when prints and media mirror life!
I close my eyes and imagine the architecture and beauty of words,
Ahhh....
my hands are up with all admiration,
parents who raise their child/children, (Y'all)
couples and singles, (Some of Y'all)
people in robes, in veil or with nothing to gain,
Those who leave their homes with pain in their heart, for better future or for other roots.
altogether,
they create the greatest talent of all,
Love for everyone, love made in Heaven!

On Board the Korean Airline.

Dreams Are Dreams

To dream of dreams that never were,
To enjoy past scenes which passed,
To want to be what could have been,
To imagine life wishfully as a truthful lie.

Move on with faces seemingly familiar.
Hear the music as if it will never end.
Smile and play with every child
There are defined limits of dreams!

Will I wait to see beyond what's real?
Shall I continue to smile to a stranger?
Do I wake up daily to expect someone?
Are there thorns with the bed of roses?

Drink every drop of boxed 'Sangria'!
Dance with the 'Little Mix' and 'Abba'!
Let the 'Fool of lights' white up the yard!
Grab every second and breath air!

(Revised)

Day 52 / 12 November

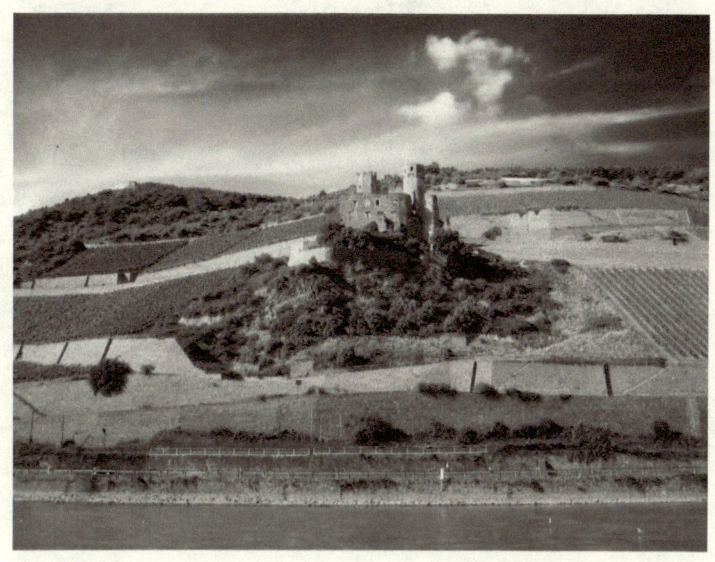

Mainz, Germany

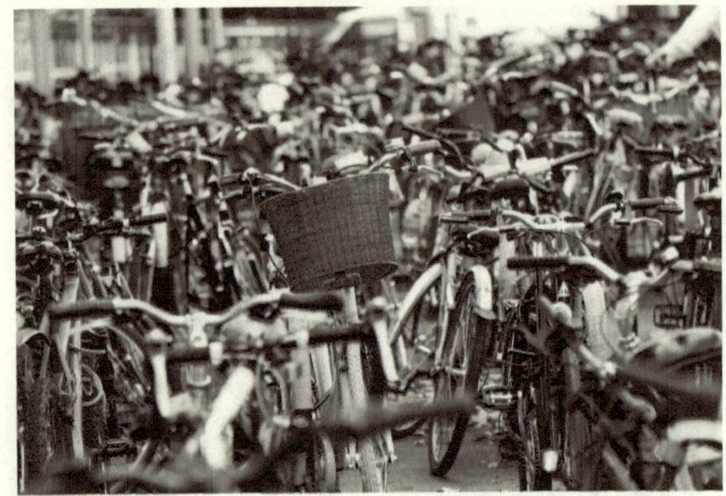

Oxford, United Kingdom

Day 53 / 13 November

Birthday's Greetings to Go

I often wonder what to do,
for special day for pals and beau?
It's so easy for families and 'Dieu',
just type the keys and click 'ditto!'!

I like to scribble a special note or two,
Sans common blood, it's family too!
Happy Birthday, 'Dearest Joan or Joe,
May you have more birthdays to go!'

Life is short, the path's long and new!
I cherished those moments long time ago
I always dream for our rendezvous!
Happy Birthday to y'all, mabuhay po kayo!

The Plato's Belief

Did we ever wonder,
why there's a day,
and a night to bear?
With sun's sparkle,
another smile,
a shade to glare?

With each step,
a right and a leap,
for the left to heap?

When I looked for one,
with luck and fate,
I found no one?
As others swayed,
like a blade of grass,
it's a love in circle!

Was Plato coached,
by Venus or Eros,
with a heart of words?

For us, for y'all halves,
carry on with Plato's heed,
find THE ONE to be one!

Day 54 / 14 November

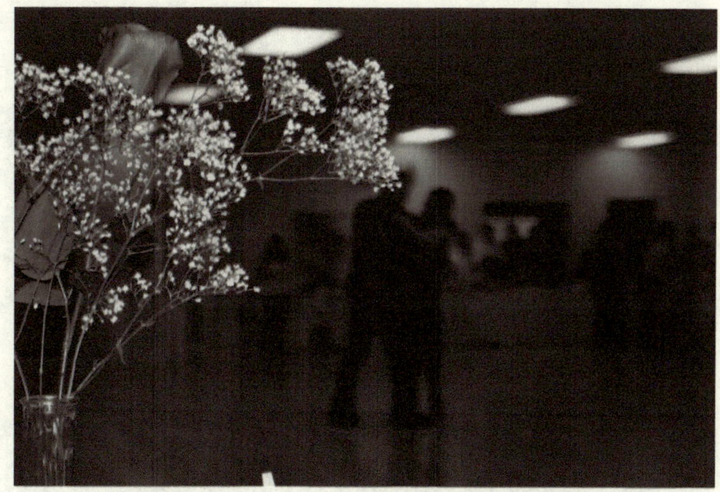

Hamilton, Ontario, Canada

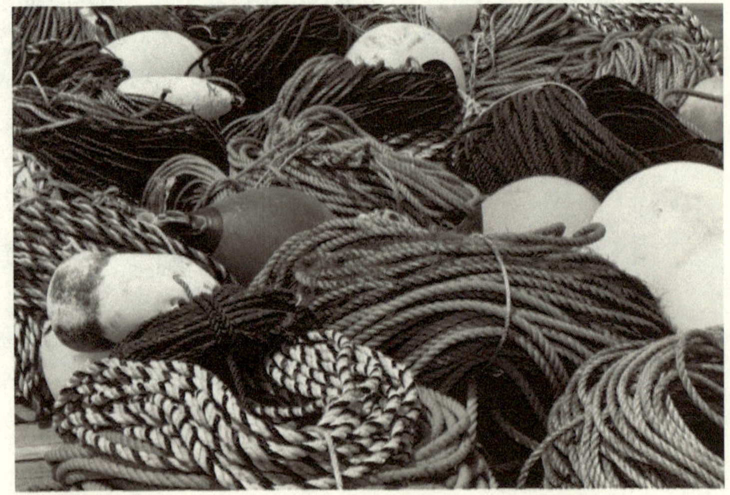

Halifax, Nova Scotia, Canada

Day 55 / 15 November

Un Jour N'est Pas Perdu

(Pour Chermayne)

Amidst the fields of gray,
Silent, nothing to see!
From the earth, lo! a speck,
Was it a twig? a fig?

Plain, barren as it is,
A book without pages.
Music with a sole pitch.

A day of sunshine waits!
Uneven hands stood still.
As the granddad's chimes ring.
Skies lit as angels fly,
Time moves on and y'all smile!

It's A New Day Tomorrow

A great year had passed
Which memories will last?
Wine, friends or my match?
'I love Me', I just launched!

To be bitter, be angry are nuts
Don't be sad, don't fret a bust
To dream dreams, we must
Take the world in a clutch!

Build new follies on sheets,
As crisp as ashes in pleats!
Together in cadence will set,
As we all march to meet!

A new day, a new year!
A new world, we all yearn!
Look up, young one or senior,
A new challenge, we'll bear!

Let's run a marathon!
Let's cast a line to fish a ton!
Let's fly a plane to Mt. Zion!
Let's revel, we'll never be alone!

Happy new year to y'all!

Day 56 / 16 November

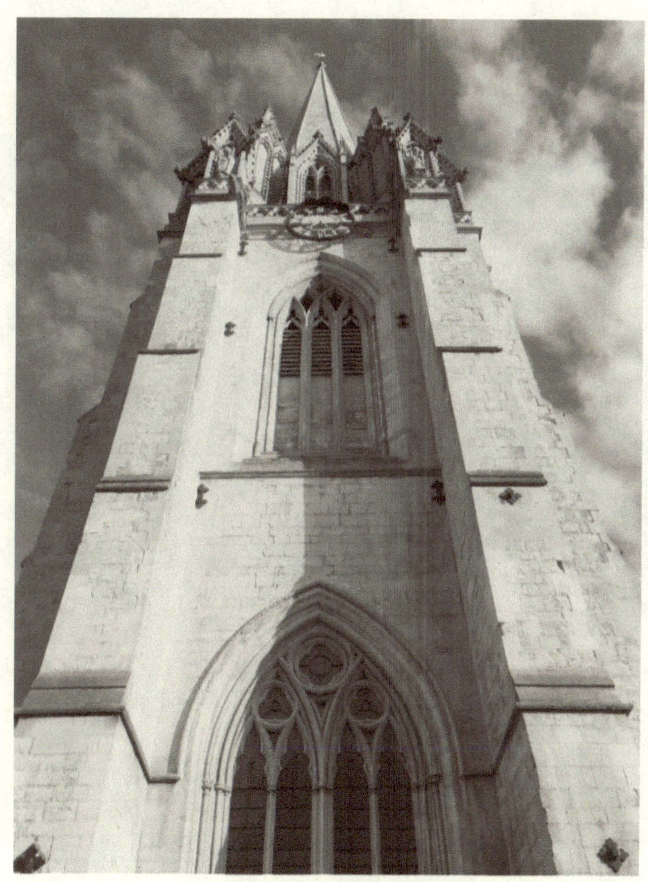

Oxford, United Kingdom

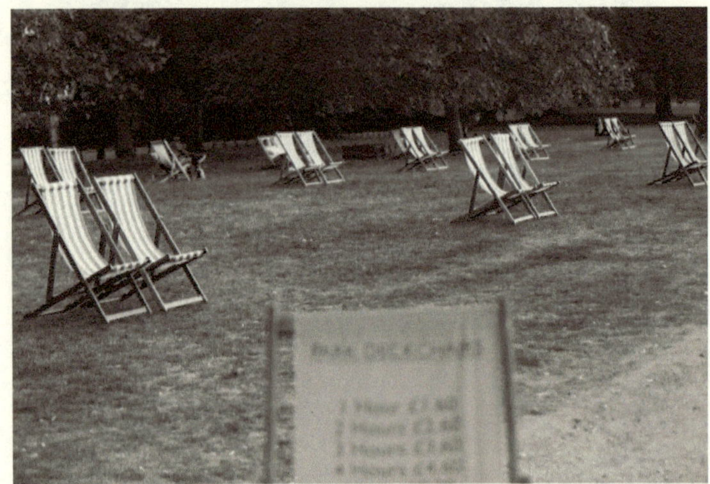

Oxford, United Kingdom

Day 57 / 17 November

Random thoughts as Requested by Amy S.
Bethel House, Dumaguete February 3, 2019

The Family of Class (84)

As I saw the salty waves,
the rushing falling waters,
the rising of the amiable sun,
I pondered on what lies ahead!

Saw the smiles, looked at faces,
t'was exactly 35 paces afar!
From the far end of the galaxy,
stood at the small island among isles!

Who are these gorgeous men?
Have I missed out these pretty women?
Was I blind and maimed,
when the world of clay molded them?

Felt joy as I trod on the burning sands,
was drowned by the ecstasy of warmth,
gasped with aroma of deep friendship,
can I hold this world to a standstill?
We have families by blood and names
tied and embraced by double strands
This unique group of men and women
Truly a magnificent one, a family of class! //

Enjoy the rest of the island tour /hopping. My spirit stays with y'all!

Thanks again!

The Woman Behind the Smile

I looked at the shadows
As grim as the furrows!
Tried to avoid the sorrow,
From that day until tomorrow!

Pulled him up many times.
Saw her smile every time!
So bright, it rings as a chime!
Tastes like a vodka with a lime?

As the moon weds the sun,
And coldness creeps me one,
The thunder gave us a loud bang,
And our tears held back as a dam!

The lady with a smile stood there,
As heaven's doors closed asunder.
Her beauty and poise stayed firm!
Ohh, I wish all women are like her!

*(*A lovely couple was shattered by the spouse's multiple brain surgeries from stroke from abnormal blood vessels. Once recovered, he went back to his previous professional practice. For years, he endured chronic headache. Just recently, I felt so helpless, when she called me to tell that he shot himself fatally leaving his lovely wife, who never lose her smile through those past years!)*

Day 58 / 18 November

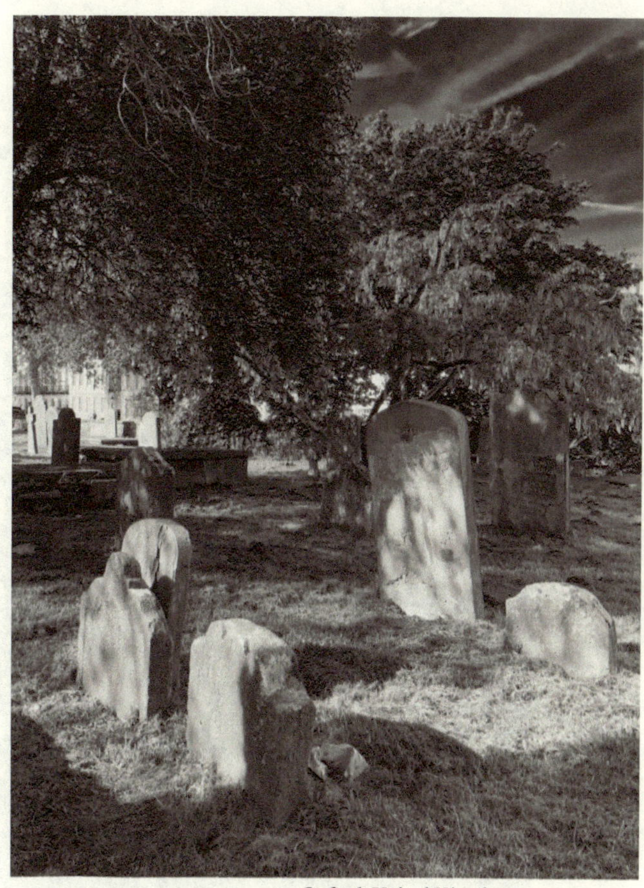

Oxford, United Kingdom

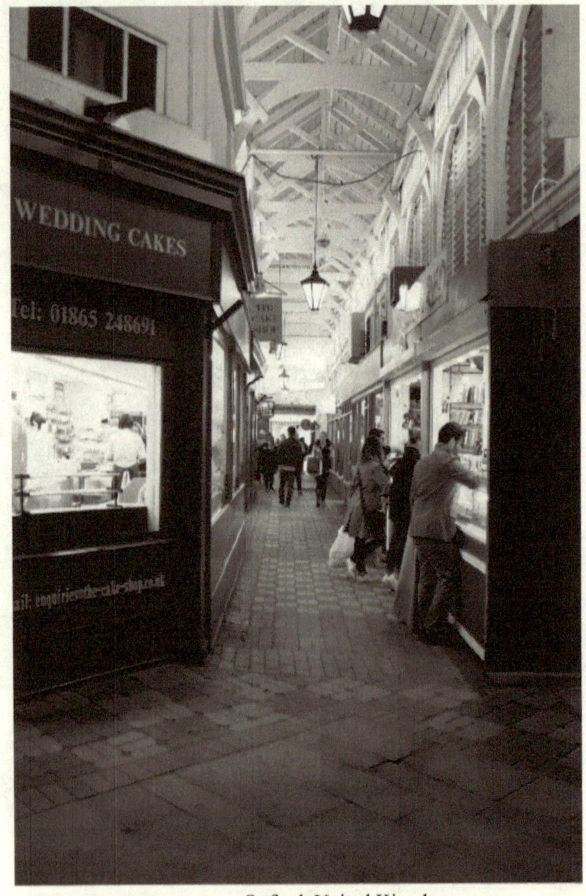

Oxford, United Kingdom

Day 59 / 19 November

Wedding Anniversary Song

(B. C. Baronia – Lyrics
Madam Ester Locson - Music)
January 26, 2017

Dueto ng Pagmamahal (Love Duet)
A> ang sabi ni itay...(solo - husband)
"Para kang diyosang may sikat sa paligid. (13)
You're like a goddess that brightens the world around us.
Ang panakaw kong sulyap na nagmamasid,(12)
My stolen glance, a searching gaze, all for you
humantong sa kapalarang tayo ay pinagbigkis.(15)
This could be destiny, our very own; we're here bound as one
Ako'y nagbigkas, mahal kita, di ako magtatangis."(16)
I said, I love you and with you, I will never be unhappy

B> ang sabi ni inay...(solo - wife)
"Napansin mo ba ang kislap sa aking mga mata?(15)
Did you see, did you ever wonder why my eyes sparkle?
sa iyong pananalita, talo pa ang makata (15)
With your loving words, ah you beat them all, you're my greatest bard!
Halos panabay nating tinanggap ang himala,(14)
And together, we declare truly this is miracle.
Binigkas ko rin, mahal kita, ito'y aking panata!" (16)
I uttered too, "I love you, that's my covenant now and always."

C> Dueto ni itay at ni inay...(Duet- husband and wife)
Animanpung taon mula noon hanggang ngayon,(14)
Through this time, sixty long years, ever lasting 'til we die
pagmamahalan natin, higit pa sa tarik ng Mayon.(16)
This love, yes our love, is far greater than the peak of Mt Mayon!
Ating pagsasama bibilang pa ng maraming taon.(16)
Together as one, we'll endure the years, a lasting time, my love
Sa awit ng pag-ibig, sasayaw tayo habang panahon!" (17)
With this Song of Love, let it play; we will dance together forever.

The Singularity of Nature

The tempest howled in awry.
The winds blown east in anger!
As I stood with hope yonder.
The arms reach towards there!
Not their ardent wish nor fear
Like an avalanche to bear!

Look at the flowers in bloom!
They swayed away from the moon.
The marching armies in doom,
All dead tired, weary they swoon.
Y'all look up and feel the sun!
Two mothers' Nature, one son!

Day 60 / 20 November

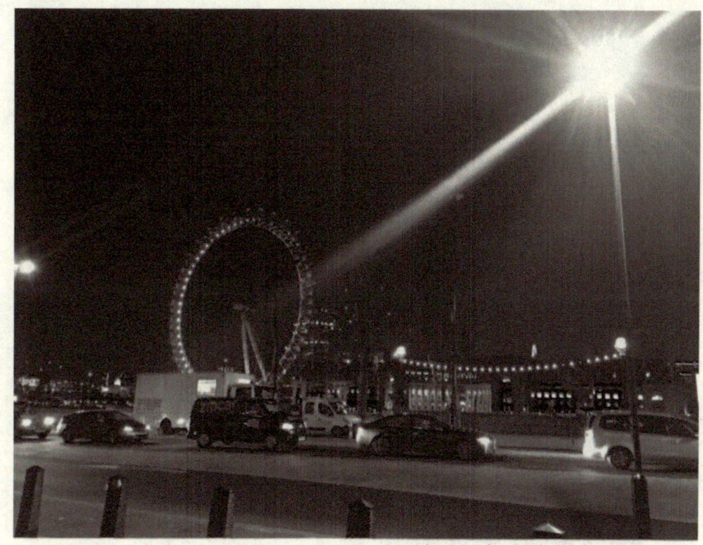

London, United Kingdom

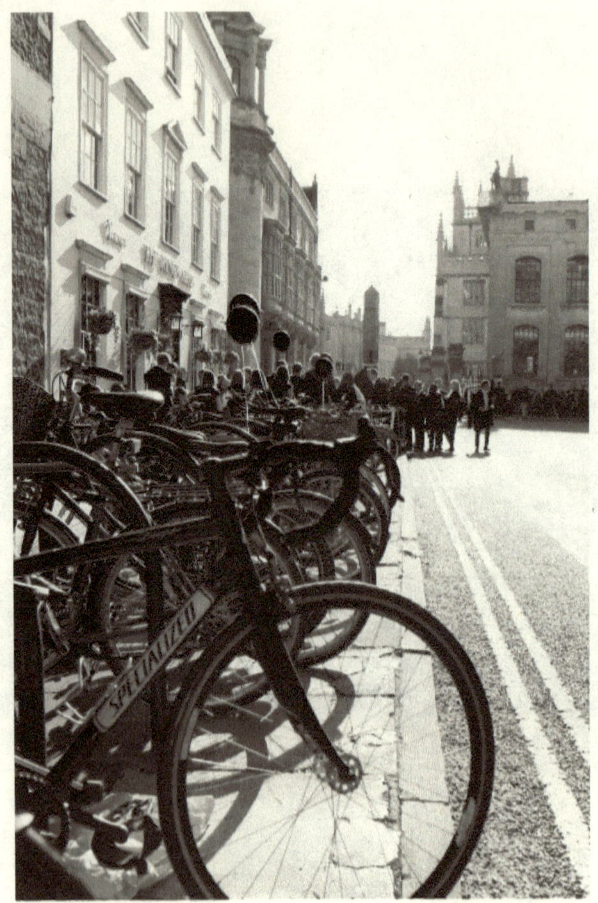

Oxford, United Kingdom

Day 61 / 21 November

Thanks. It's skull based, one of my first loves.

My Random Thoughts

To a Dearest Student

Enjoy and learn.
Live life to its fullest.
Don't sing 'I dreamed
the dream'.
But walk the dream
like no one else!
Life is short!
Live fairly as others.
Love everyone as He does!
Smile and laugh, have fun,
As I see you walk
towards your dream!

Sister Ade

Now that I know 27 years ago,

That radiant smile we still woo,

I can't help wonder, we can't let go.

The happiness

Day 62 / 22 November

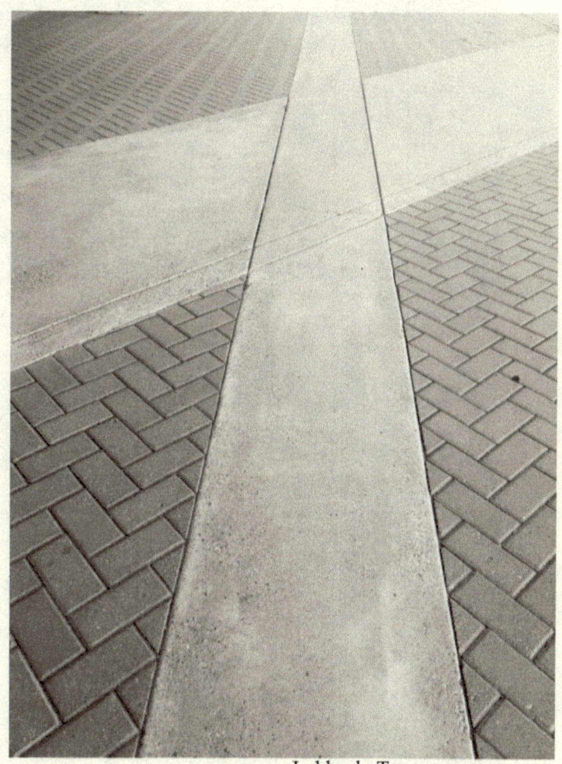

Lubbock, Texas

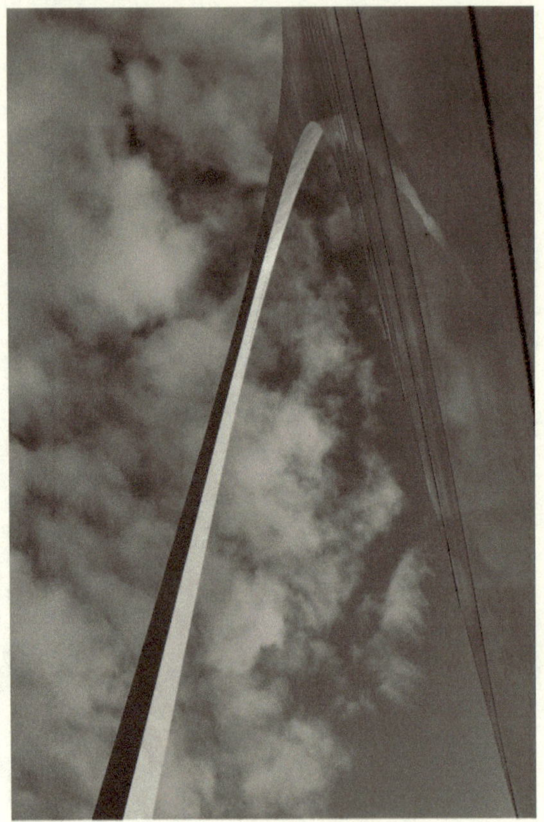

St. Louis, Missouri

Day 63 / 23 November

A Time Stopper

(As the Rainbow Drew Her in)
Let me ride the carriage of time.
Let the bee's toil foil those oily hands.
Let those bells be mute and muffled.
And let the tiny beads be one!

I faced my dream when am awake.
I ran my ambition in fast stride.
I mused each day as yesterday.
And wished today will never end.

She played the square keys with a smile.
She left and fizzled, to be back as grizzle.
She's here, yet breathes the northern air.
She could be, would she? shouldn't be?

I drove and grazed as musical notes fly.
I wondered at the realm of zeroes and one
I realized a silver image with my glance.
I'll keep her entrenched with my sight.

Just as the river sways with my unyielding sands,
birds and bees see pollens from each end.
Both of us will leave four marks on our path,
as the horizon fades, our footsteps part.

Ahh, as the moon tries to hide it's half,
the feathers of the skies dim the North one.
Let me then sing a Brahms's for Venus.
As time stopped, it filled up my happy sac.

Bb minus
23 Oct 2017

Niagara

Amidst the foggy and drizzly night,
I stumbled and grabbed a fig in sight,
Never thought it was good enough
Made me stood up and led me back.

I stayed up and wondered still glazed,
Wished among the gods and saints,
That I can continue to move along
In this path

Day 64 / 24 November

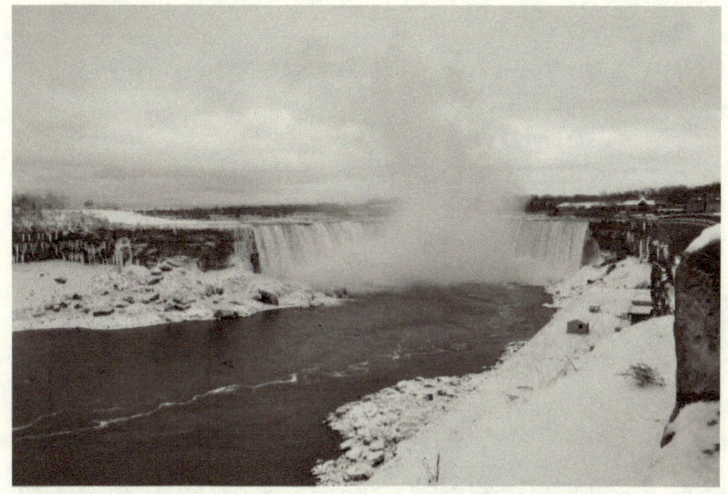

Niagara Falls, Ontario, Canada

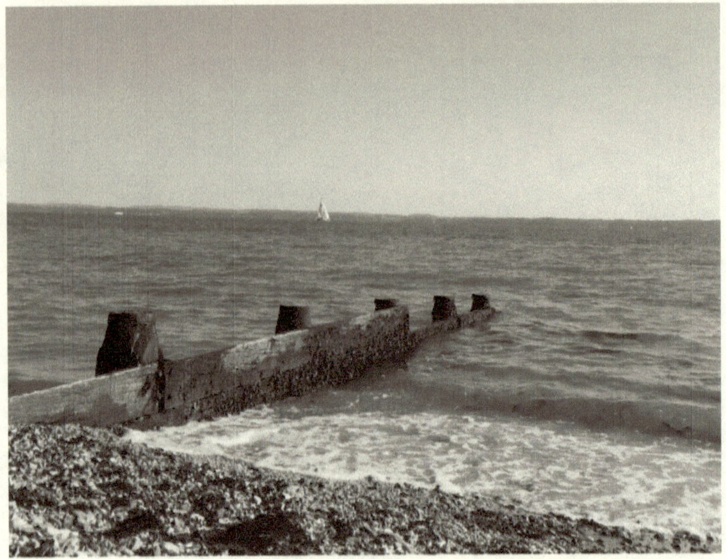

English Channel, United Kingdom

Day 65 / 25 November

What to Do / Que Faire?

Each travel puts me in a spin!
Here I bought L tickets and dream.
Cast a reel and wish for a big one!
Took a vantage seat and ogle
Gorgeous curve bottoms and
Helens, Brads of Troy

Let Me Be Free

We share the laughter and fun,

The joy of ne'er ending band,

of music and men,

of strings and dames!

Day 66 / 26 November

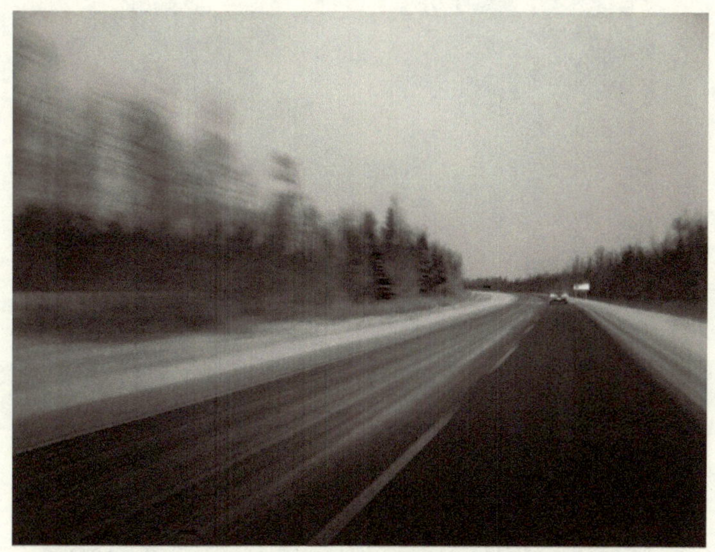

Ottawa, Ontario, Canada

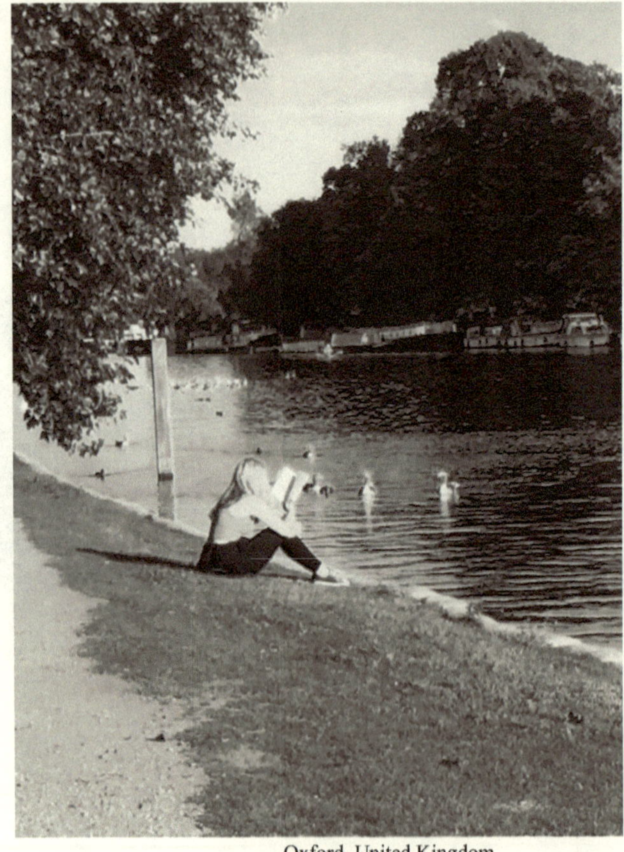

Oxford, United Kingdom

Day 67 / 27 November

The Girl from Tennessee

Good morning my lady,
An old-fashioned Dame,
Hugs and kisses for thee,
They won't hurt, you'll see!

As you're proud to be,
An American in horsey,
A dear old kin signee,
With a famous relic to see!

What are you? A tots' molder!
Who are you? All men's dear!
Where are you? At a barn yonder!
How are you? A dreamer to discover!

With all the king's men out there,
A town crier with a scroll, sneers!
Not even for knights or paupers,
Who am I to sit at the iron chair?

With a chuckle to remember,
A deafening cordless laughter,
Too far to trot, so fly to be near,
the Girl from Tennessee, let's rock!

An Expression Too Far

(From a Man I Saw Love)

From the isles off grid,
To a no-time zone stead,
Settled to a heavenly abode,
Was amazed, a salad of words!

Enchanté, Buongiorno!
Danke Schön, Salamat Po!
Hola, am glad to see you!
Auf Wiedersehen, Te amo !

Out of bounds, a sober meet.
An urgent work, a usual routine.
At the OR table, took out the gbm*
And casually, I spoke with the man!

The first encounter, a senior couple.
But what he said, all in me trembled!'
"Been with her since I was thirteen,
I wished I could have been her!"

gbm - most aggressive / malignant brain tumor*

Day 68 / 28 November

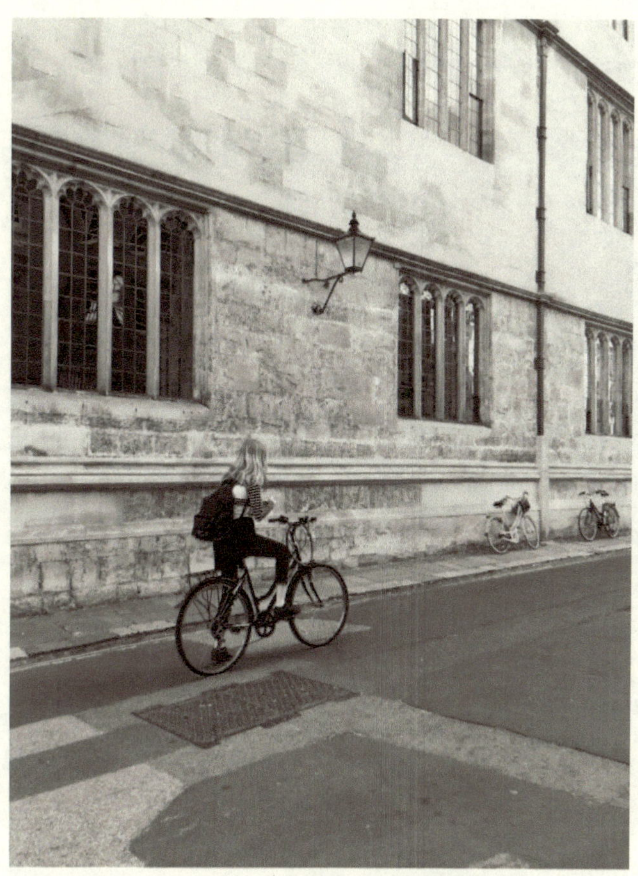

Oxford, United Kingdom

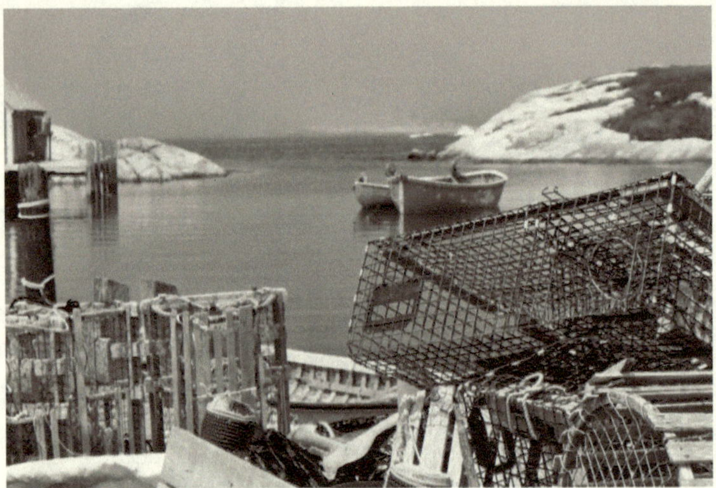

Halifax, Nova Scotia, Canada

Day 69 / 29 November

What is a Friend?

He's a brother!
She's a sister!
Maybe older!
Maybe younger!
Like a twin-ner!
The blood is thicker!
Ours, a lot better together!

Let's Play Football (Not Soccer)

When Am Old!

Fear not, my loved one!
You're on your own!
Stand up and look beyond
The future is not gone!

Prove those tales to be true!!
Count the blessings to grow!
Bless the world with your glow!
Don't look back with sorrow!
While my bones crackled as I walk,
With Broca's stroke, am unable to talk,
And the thief C knocks, I can't balk!
When am old, am happy am still a 'hulk!"

The stuff I learned will be gone!
Whatever I left, the will is done!
Just throw me the pigskin as a stone,
I'll breeze with fun to the end zone!

Day 70 / 30 November

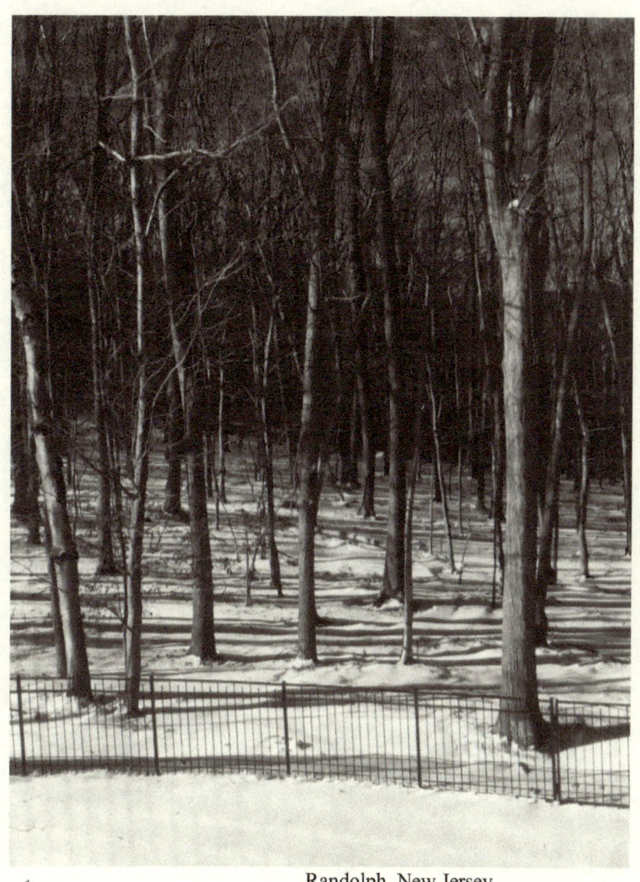

Randolph, New Jersey

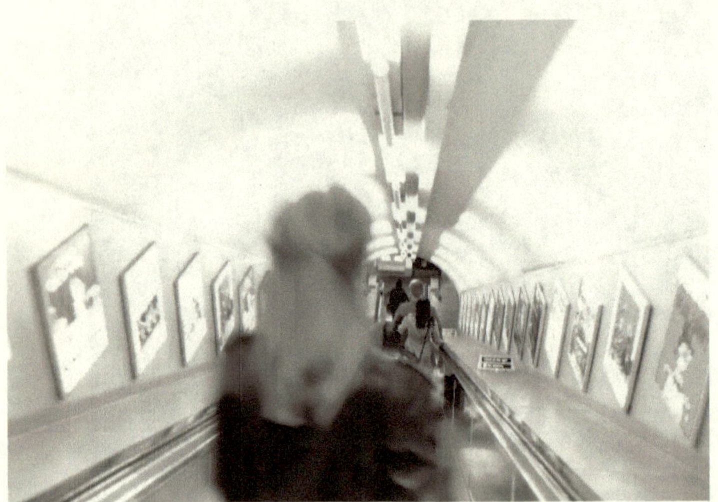

London, United Kingdom

Day 71 / 01 December

Dulce of 84

A Helen of Troy
Those Ships ahoy!
A Regal lady,
Our eyes wonder!
Her beauty shines
Is ‘L’ before ‘C’?
But we like best-
That ‘c’ before ‘L’!
Like the sun each day,
Cold warmth at dawn,
Ohh. a gorgeous one!
Amidst those long years,
Her face, a Portrait for life,
A marvelous Kathy-like!
The Dulce of ‘84!

"Tony R."

Smile like Mona Lisa!
Inherit the 'pinoy saya'!
With no, pain, with all the stamina,
The Laughter's at Pamplona!

We'll see one, like no other,
It's unique, I thought it's a sneer!
the feelings but exude laughter,
That's our Tony followed with an R!

Day 72 / 02 December

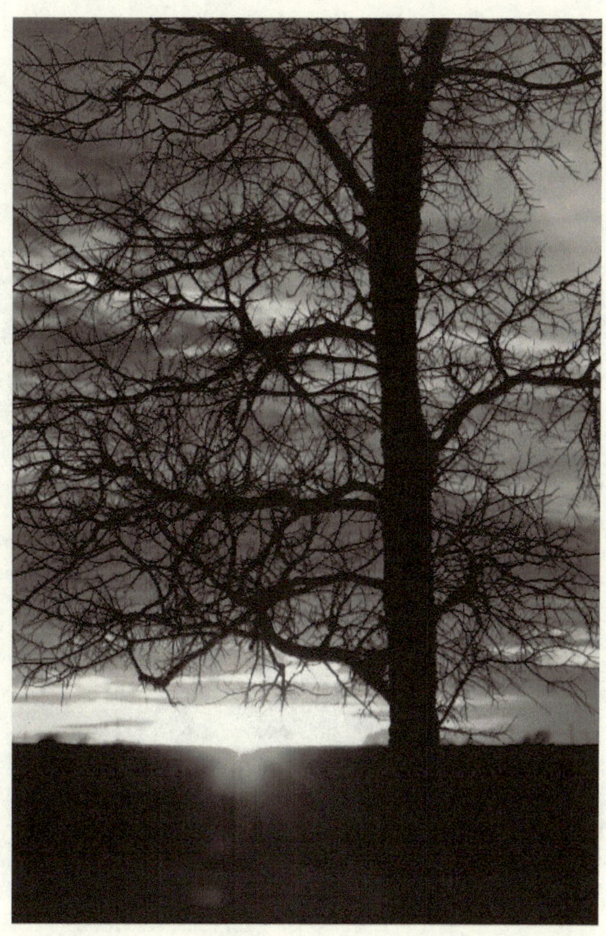

Lubbock, Texas

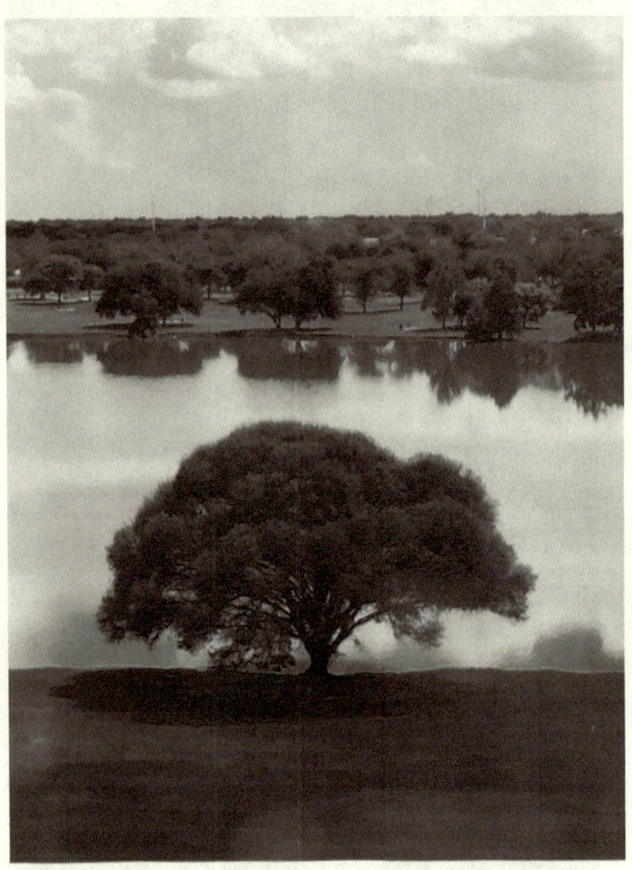

Lubbock, Texas

Day 73 / 03 December

The Perfect Seat

I travelled far and wide
To see the world at a glance
Ventured into a grad school,
Now, flew in with Mac and mobile!

Long hours hadn't changed!
Prior check in with TSA, a must!
Shoes and belt should be handy,
Like fluids, one can gulp with ease!

Business class will be nice,
Y'all arrived the same time though.
So, is it a 27D or an F? an aisle I like most!
To sit with someone like you, doesn't matter, it's still the best!

Christmas @ Home is Fun

As I scanned those digital pics
with lovely faces and smiles,
the past cherished moments
went flashed back in time!

Retro checkered shirts,
and wide bottom pants,
Elevator shoes, palm-wide ties,
And converse high cuts abound!

Gyrating hips, with raised arms,
Was it YMCA or banyuhay?
"Dang-it", I cried with 'Anak!'
Ne'er mind, let's chicken dance?!

I forgot how we swing!
Today's mislabeled terms,
My apologies, there's no app!
With Alexa and Siri, Google wins!

With today's time, the world shrinks!
With Facebook, Twitter, all is quick as cereal!
So, I won't miss anything, please email me,
Christmas @ home is fun!

Day 74 / 04 December

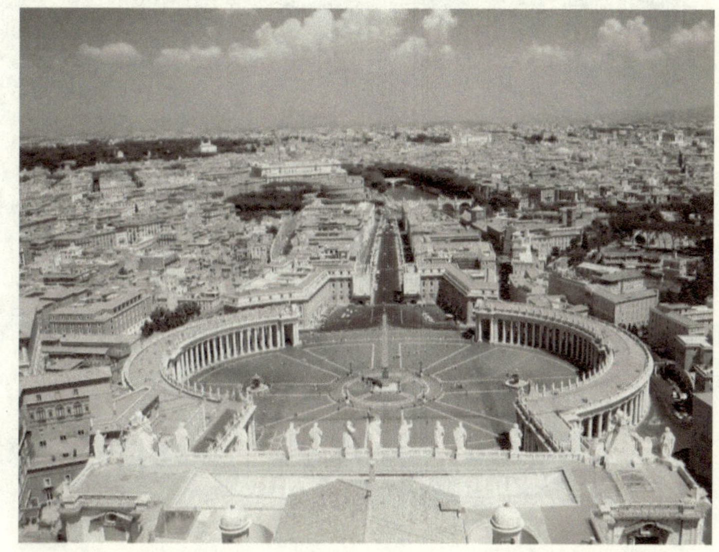

Vatican, Italy

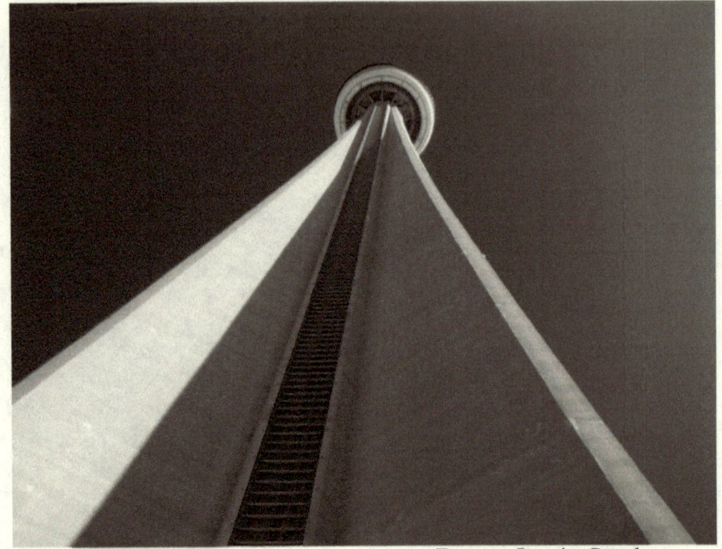

Toronto, Ontario, Canada

Day 75 / 05 December

Am Here Yet am Not!

As I read thru those lines
As you describe someone,
I look at myself and asked,
Is it me? a long-awaited fate?

As I read thru those lines
As you describe yourself,
I looked up at the heaven,
"Thank you, my wait is done!"

Medusa's Golden Hair

Every flight I looked around,
every seat I tried to reserve,
every food I ate and chomped,
every music I am charmed,

I saw the silhouette of Medusa!
Her golden hair once admired,
then her true colors opened out.
Thank G--, the gate control closed!

With writhing but painless sore,
Black clouds loomed the past,
Ballads played one base higher
And Mona Lisa's unfocused smile.

Thank the wedding I had walked,
Ironically not as the bride's groom,
As one of those 'experts' couples.
T'was a dog tail's wag cut Medusa's hair!

Day 76 / 06 December

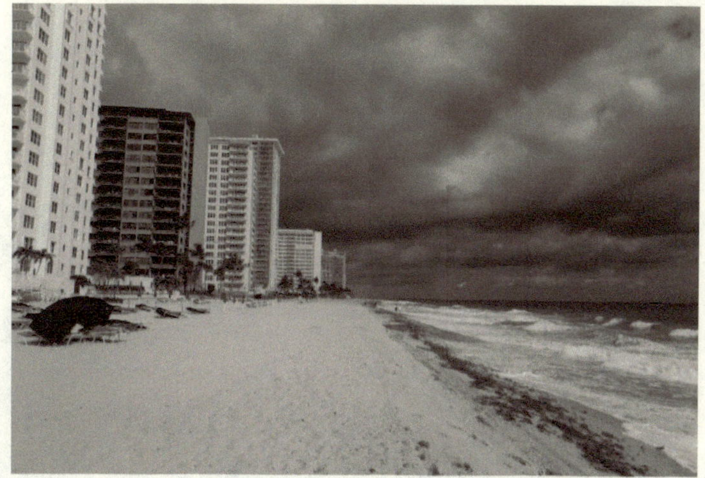

Fort Lauderdale, Florida

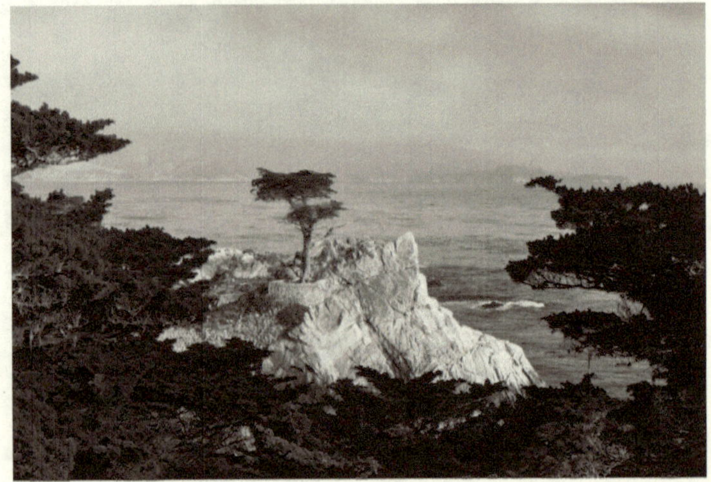

California State Route 1, California

Day 77 / 07 December

I Am What I Am

Two roses in a row,
Poked deeply as I sow.
Time and effort as duo,
Put my ego to a low!

Why do men weep
As they walk deep?
A lot of thorns to keep,
A Mountain to leap?

Go on and let go
See what to see
Hear all about her,
Say yes, none to no!
LOL, I am what I am,
One step, I'm damned!
Buzz of bees, be mum!
"Lest you stick like a gum!"

**Random thoughts when I heard and was struck profoundly by a casual remark from a TV anchor and I quote.*

Can Shadows Stay?

"We Are Only Good as What We Left Behind!"

//Can Shadows Stay?

Looking around, I see.
What the world I had,
the tirades we voiced,
the prize we all goad!

Pages and pages I've read!
To turn raven those empty dots!
To adore the sound of gold!
To tread on green crisp moat!

Let the womb bloat!
The cries turned into sighs!
Saved those teary foreheads,
as we toiled, we dread!

And when the moon sleeps,
the sun sets in the east,
the shadows we cast,
Can they stay and not passed? //

Day 78 / 08 December

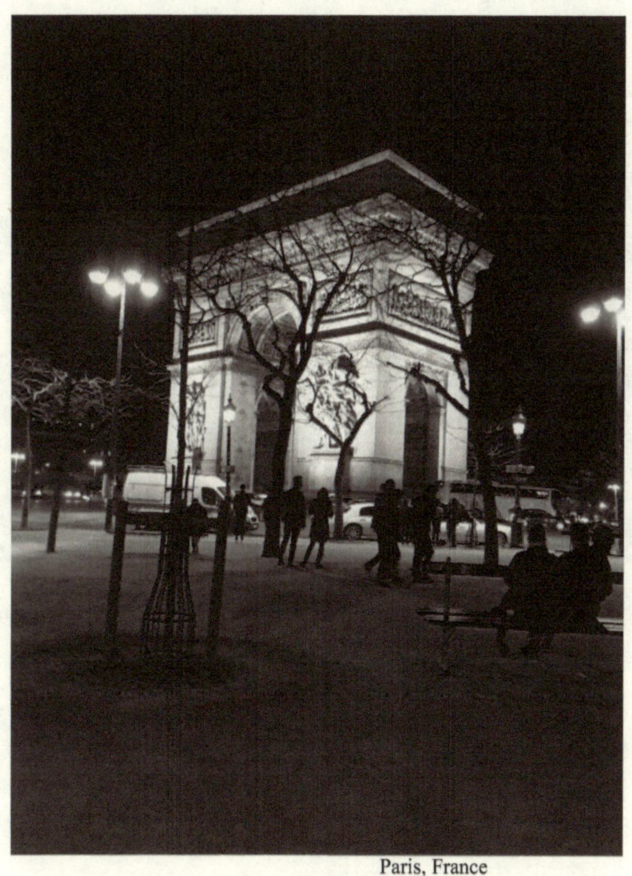

Paris, France

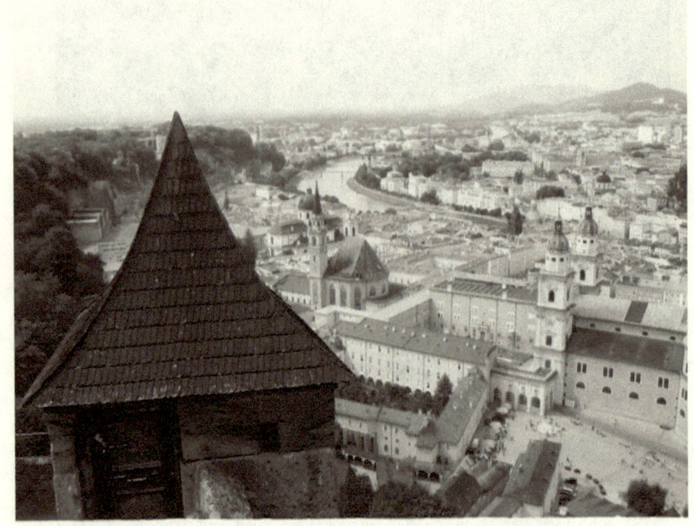

Salzburg, Austria

Day 79 / 09 December

Aboard JAL 745

The Southern Lights

I like to see those brilliant lights,
As I travel north with freezing cold,
Dancing like angels with muted sound,
Like vanishing jewels on holy ground

For half a century,
I wandered like a fly,
Each time, each day,
Looking for a fresh pie!

Three wacycles

Smile Behind the Man

Go ahead and glance!
Let those times roll,
amidst this great smile,
are secrets beyond keep

No muted silence to be heard,
Not a pin drop to get startled,
Any music note fell on any clef,
Just a hustle and rustle to enjoy!

I wonder how can I be
A man, no woman can aspire
Just a friend y'all desire.
Like a pup, to pet like a Yorkie!

Day 80 / 10 December

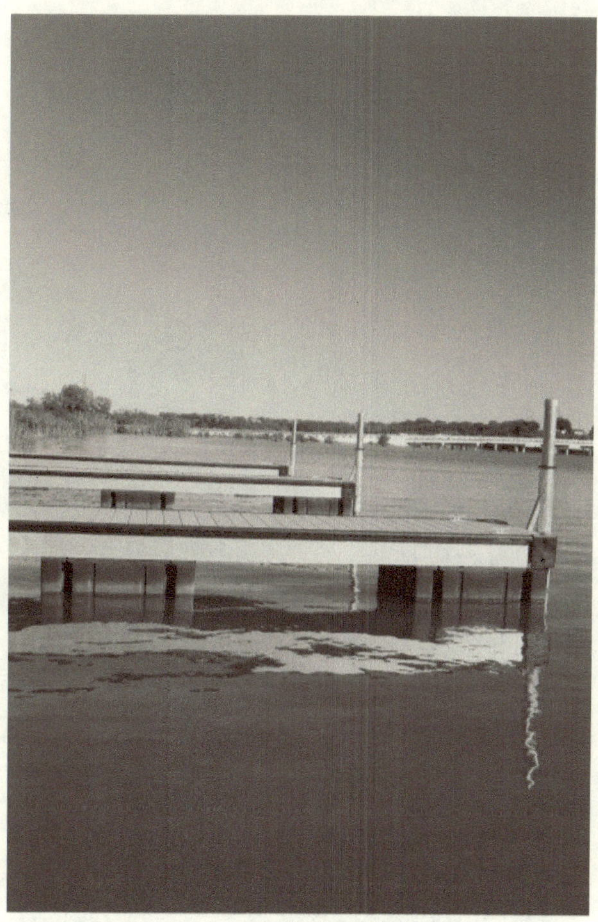

Granbury, Texas

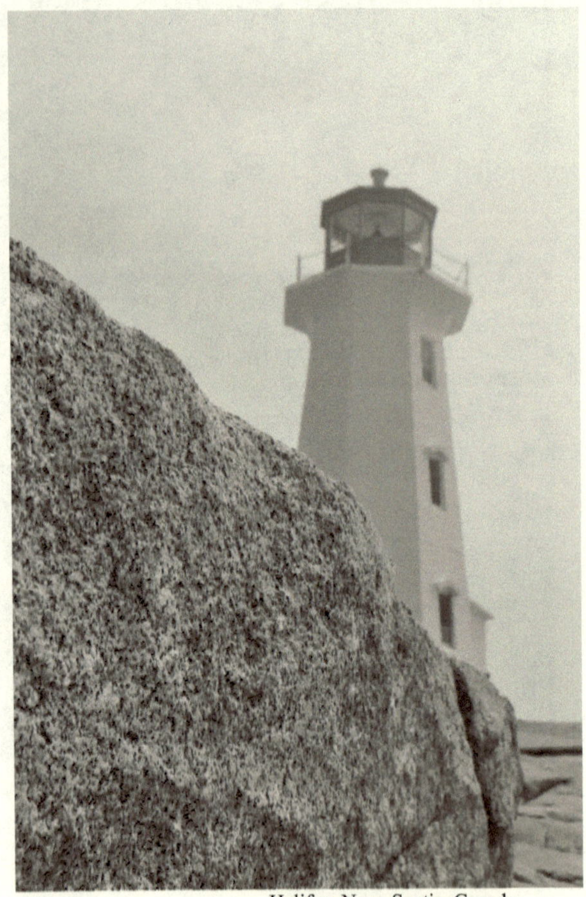

Halifax, Nova Scotia, Canada

Day 81 / 11 December

On Death

It's a word unlike nothing,
A certainty left to unbearing,
Feared by few while I remain,
A continuum and an end!

It comes in many ways.
Seen it, petrified!
Sighed when with big C,
Felt uneasy with intent!

Fear not, life well-trodden!
Heed the rule as golden.
Love all men/women!
Even aim high, be Like HIM!

As lines and sounds mix,
from looking at par
to walking at lull,
the date is cast!

Cherish the best times!
Cry or laugh with tears,
We're here as lilies grow,
From waters which ne'er dry!

Let's breath the same air,
Re-step in each stair,
We sing with all the flair,
Like no one had went over.

Nothing should end,
No one can be invisible,
Let those memories linger
As their spirits guide!
When our hour turns night,
And our dear ones' minutes,
Don't glance like Lot's Edith,
Behold, stare with glare like stars!

(My Random thoughts - to fear something inevitable, it's better, to treat is as laughable!)

Shall I Fear You, The Big C?

Out of nowhere,
it's great as a stalker!
It's not a oner,
just a double dealer!

Is it with the family?
Too much? Too sunny?
With cool spirits, or being sexy,
Or as a fireless Smokey?

As the card faces up,
the two strands gallop,
the heart's in 'lubbi-dup',
and the mind gets dope!

when babies cry,
as adults deny,
and parents defy,
I look with glazy eye!

This is my story!
I'll write it as most cheery,
With my friends and family,
Like each day is an eternity!

Day 82 / 12 December

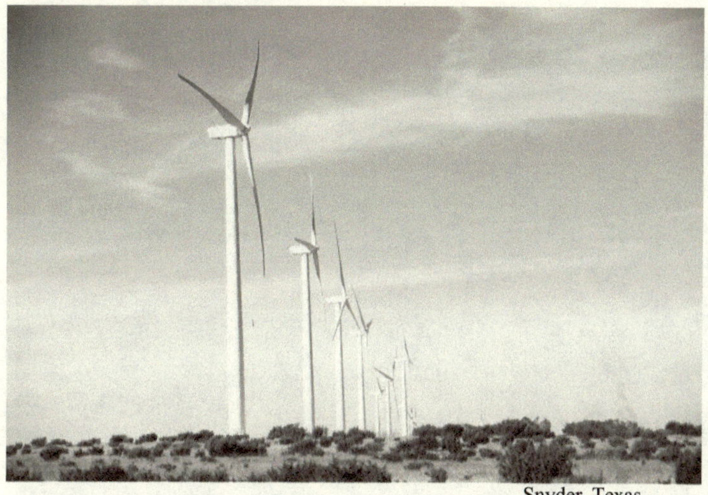

Snyder, Texas

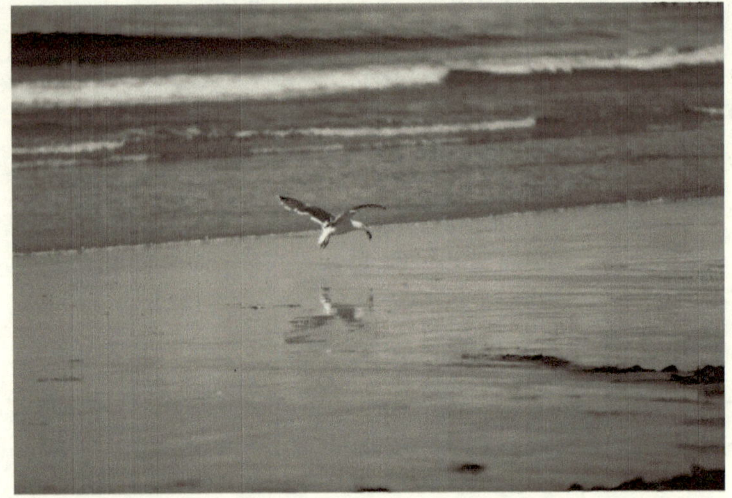

Balboa, California

Day 83 / 13 December

Was That a Dream?

The day was tainted brown,
As I floated with a wet gown,
Nothing much to go down,
With boredom, I had to frown!

With a run of zeroes and ones,
A lady with a great smile yawned,
She giggled, laughed and chuckled,
The A&B Gas scale, “T’was a great one!”

With the sound of staccatos,
to a world I’ve never been before,
With the tempest on the horizon,
I felt it was spring in autumn!

Hold back the sands of Persia!
Turn the sun’s rays to fuchsia!
A new day with my owl’s eyes,
Was that a dream? I looked daze!

Merry Xmas to Y'all

I looked at the past
With my backside
Had asked myself
I did things different?

Kept my promises?
Healed someone?
Paid my dues?
Made others laugh?

Cried with pain?
Sighed with failure?
Ignored a friend?
Unloved a stranger?

With all the 'wars'
We endured each day,
Let's be merry always
For Christmas is daily!

Day 84 / 14 December

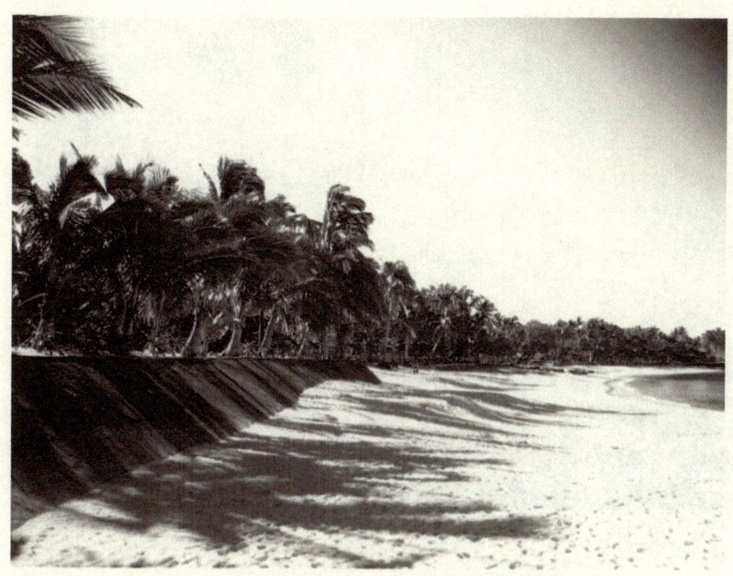

Pagudpud, Ilocos, Philippines

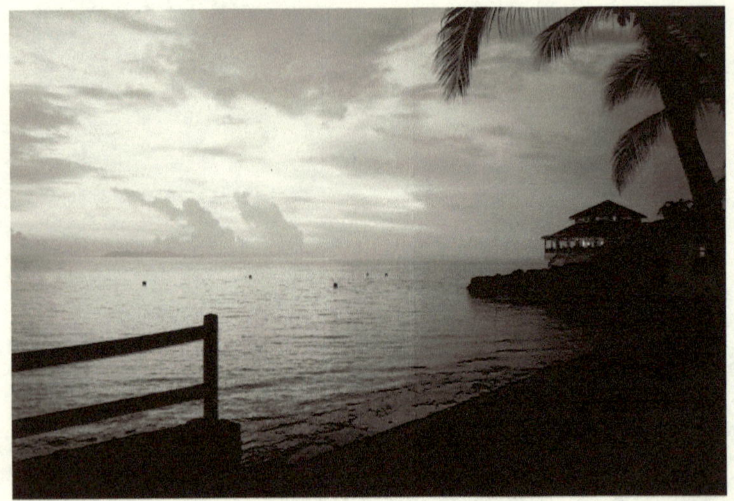

Anilao, Batangas, Philippines

Day 85 / 15 December

A Trilogy at Dawn

(Dearest Helen, our classmate, we all pray for you. God Bless you and may you Rest in Peace!)

I. How Do I Pray for you?
Will I close my eyes and weep?
As I reminisce those times to keep
Your smile, your voice, too meek
As we all bear the roads we seek.

II. How do I remember thee?
Shall I retrace the steps thru the sands,
And lend the day's moon a hand?
Perhaps, sing your songs with the band,
So, our voice and your notes to bond?

III. How do I let go?
Will I tread on with a heavy heart?
On a path with a faceless crowd?
I'd rather hold the world to a standstill
As we all look to the skies with a smile!

A Flashback in Time

I looked at the sunset.
For each day, I sat,
with an environ too hot
Nothing to

I knew where you were,
Followed the news with fear
We all knew where we bear
It will be now, soon or later

Day 86 / 16 December

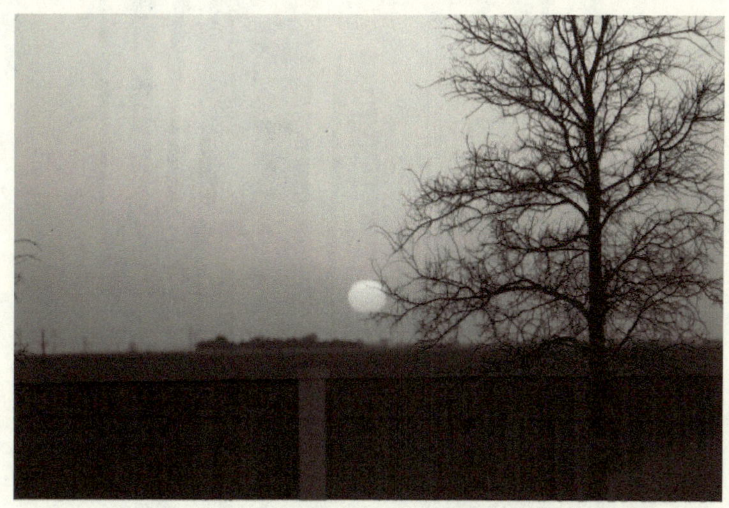

Lubbock, Texas

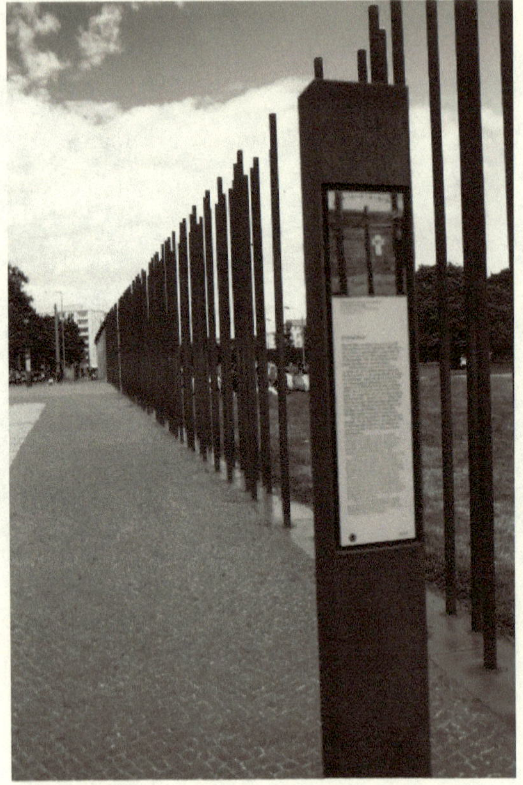

Berlin, Germany

Day 87 / 17 December

"Noli Me Tangere"

(In English, Touch Me Not)

Let me tweet you my chum,
as I read your Instagram,
E mail me as I heat up my bum,
Let's text or video chat to charm?

I hunger for your touch!
as we lay on the couch!
I miss your raspy voice,
live music and your poise!

Is the Ball Round?

*(*A question I asked due to the past agony of defeat with a beamy hope of the future)*

Play tough on an uphill shinny*,
Be among the sixteen, my sweetie!
Don't stop to be the elite eight- yeah!
To be at the final four, don't hurry!

Tonight is the night-y,
Are y'all inky and bloody?
Sense the red raider rider's musky?
As we rode to a game so feisty!

Stay up, don't be sleepy!
Look, the streets were so empty!
People stood firm and were sassy
Five minutes were an eternity!

Is the ball round, my flatty*?
As one threw it with certainty,
While some threw it so badly?
The buzzer was so screechy!

Beware, a stroke's a possibility!
people do, from dismay and anxiety!
Today, they might had claimed that city.
Relax y'all, 2020 is ours, with surety!

And be proud for the boys, that was crafty!

**Shinny - street hockey*
**Flatty - flatmate, Brit colloq*

Day 88 / 18 December

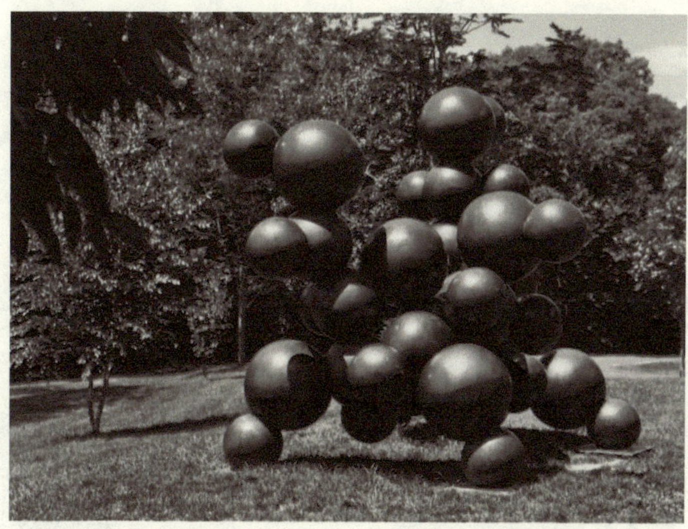

St. Louis, Missouri

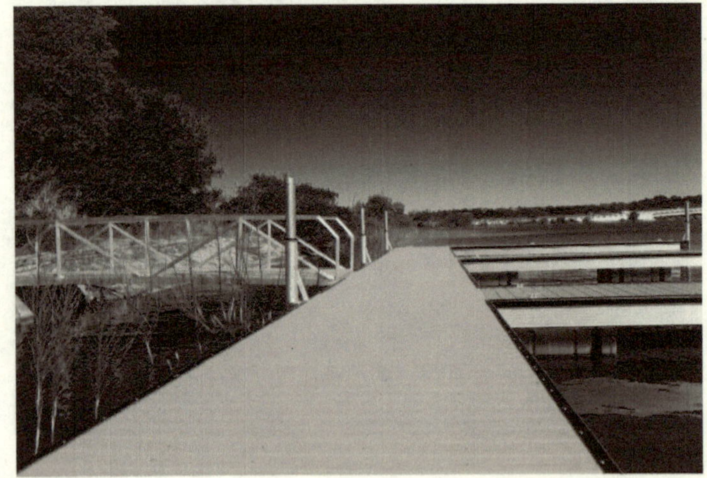

Granbury, Texas

Day 89 / 19 December

Let me share y'all my random thoughts triggered by this 'vaccine thread'

Where Do I Stand?

Will I be an edge lower?
So my chin's higher?
Will I just go above the rest,
It's no sweat as I feast?

Shall I go with the tide,
And impel with a slide?
Would it better to bide,
And reason with pride?

What's always loud,
I can be drown with a thud!
The silence I can hear,
It might be worth an ear!

'Love the least of mine',
Offer Him our genuine time!
Hurt no one as y'all detest,
'offer the other cheek' is blest!

Build towers over walls,
Be still, hear the squall!
Let fly the cotton sheets,
Stand on parallel pleats!

I'll do what's best for y'all!
I'll seek the truth over ornate halls!
I'll lie down where poison ivy crawls
I'll stand 'til am last to fall!

Love of My Life

I've looked around and wed twice
I had children from those I loved.
With stroke of faith, I had to leave
For several reasons, the usual ones?

In high school I wooed a girl for years
I didn't write a note or call for a while
So she came back, all my efforts gone
Didn't bother to look till I met the Cause!

For years, I loved and fought for them!
Just like the rest of us in youthful vigor.
Then when I saw My Dad shed a tear
Tears I had never seen, I decided to part

A woman I loved, with the same belief,
I had to live with my bourgeoise way
Out of the blue, I just met and told her
'Let's move on, I'll go separate way!

Got bored with my job and went to med
On my last years, found someone near.
This was it when Kim, our baby, arrived!
We grieved, she left, with Kim's demise!

She took away a boy, my family so loved
Taken from us, we didn't know why?
Years past, my fault not to look for him.
So now, we respect him for all his want!
For years, I live sans the love of my life!

Day 90 / 20 December

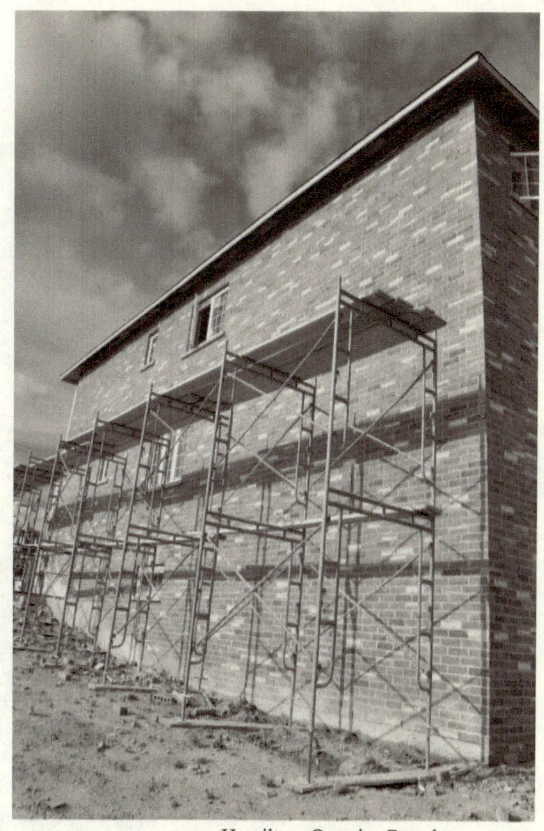

Hamilton, Ontario, Canada

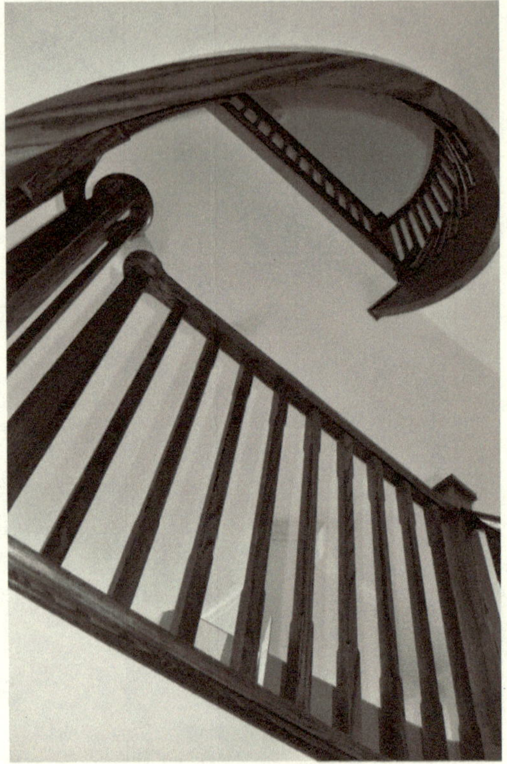

Hamilton, Ontario, Canada

Day 91 / 21 December

Le Cercle De Ma Vie

Like a youth from yesteryears with my first crush,
Like a child who dipped
one's hand on a cookie jar,
Like a birdling on its initial flight,

A sorrow when one just left,
A tear of joy with an accomplishment!
A smile of tranquility with my kids at play!
Alas, the sight of someone,
The words of her stories,
The pics of her family!

That's the turn of the other half,
In full circle, not a zigzag,
The circle of my life

Online Thing-I

It's a game of wits
A play of words
A charade of doubt
A fun of laughter
A no-drama free
A needle on a heap
A time to play
Not for men of words
Not for women to cry
A sweep on the top
A mahjong shuffle
From one to another
A hurdle on the loop
A treadmill's walk
Until a tie on the end
Or meet someone
And just say, 'hi'!

Day 92 / 22 December

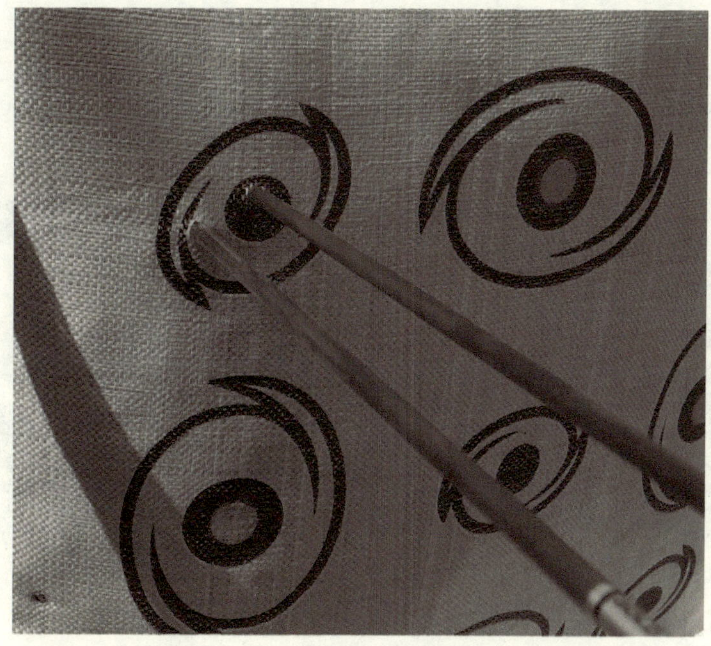

Lubbock, Texas

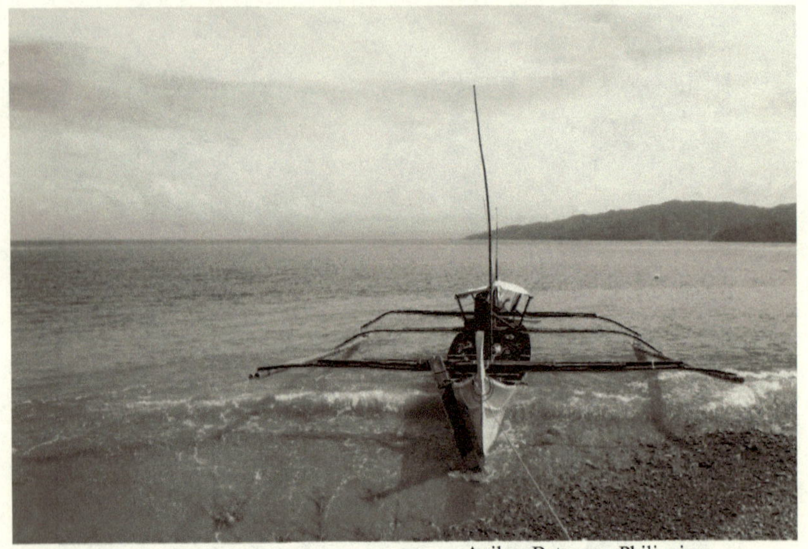

Anilao, Batangas, Philippines

Day 93 / 23 December

The Wonderful Shades of Life

(Post 23rd December Party)

Have I seen all shades of life,
As I venture and struggle each day?
Did I capture my children's smile,
as I looked thru my hassy and SLR?

Did you hear my laughter,
as I mingled with oldies and pals?
Can I tell you my feelings,
As my sibs, mom and I did a groupie?

Can you grab the time of day,
As I freeze it with Yannie and Liam?
Did you click the 'menu' button,
As we all watch Gabby and Isa had fun?
Such is my life, all shades into one,
From Kim to Jed to all the K's I love,
Keith, Kyle and Kasey and their moms.
I am alone, am happy, am ready at last!

ACKNOWLEDGEMENTS

"The Best for the Last"

Sincerest gratitude to:

Him; our dearest Dad and our angel, Kim;
my beloved children;
my wonderful mom;
sis Bee, my constant 'first' reader and critic;
my brother and sisters, for their support;
all triggers of my random thoughts,
my circles of friends and colleagues; and
to KJ Waters, for her assistance in the publication of this work.

INDEX OF TITLES

INDEX OF PHOTOS

www.ingramcontent.com/pod-product-compliance
Lightning Source LLC
LaVergne TN
LVHW090942080826
845145LV00003B/851

* 9 7 8 1 7 3 4 3 0 4 1 2 1 *